Drama in the Air

By the same author

LIFEBOATS TO THE RESCUE
THE YORKSHIRE RIPPER STORY
KLAUS BARBIE

Drama in the Air

Extraordinary True Stories of Daring and Courage

JOHN BEATTIE

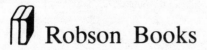 Robson Books

First published in Great Britain in 1989 by Robson Books Ltd,
Bolsover House, 5–6 Clipstone Street, London W1P 7EB

Copyright © 1989 John Beattie

British Library Cataloguing in Publication Data

Beattie, John, *1941-*
    Drama in the air.
    1. Aeroplanes. Flying-Stories, anecdotes
    I. Title
    629.132'52

ISBN 0 86051 564 8

Printed in Great Britain by Billing & Sons Ltd, Worcester

For Sue

Contents

ACKNOWLEDGEMENTS   8

FOREWORD   9

INTRODUCTION   11

1 Taff Holden – The Engineer's Nightmare   17

2 Jim Clark – The Winchman's Narrow Escape   28

3 Tom Dobney – Schoolboy Pilot   41

4 Jock Menmuir – For Those in Peril on the Sea   54

5 Joe Fusniak – The Polish Air-Gunner's Loyalty   66

6 Mike Yarwood – Disaster on the Rig   81

7 Graham Jacobs – The Parachutist's Nightmare   96

8 Jeff Todd – Hanging by a Thread   111

9 Tod Hilton – The Aussie and the Walrus   124

10 Mike Lakey – Scot of the Year   137

11 John Spencer – Diving into Darkness   149

12 Alasdair Campbell – Amateurs to the Rescue   161

13 Dave Bullock – The Courage of the Winchman   175

14 Chris Folland – Visibility Nil   186

15 The Mystery of Flight 706   199

16 Kilo–Foxtrot's Achilles' Heel   208

17 Conflict on Flight BE 548   216

Acknowledgements

I should like to place on record my gratitude – and admiration – for all the brave airmen who spent so much time with me, re-living the dramatic events you will find chronicled in this book. Seeing 'how it was' through someone else's eyes is not easy and, almost inevitably, there will be errors. If so they are wholly mine and not those of the men who so patiently tried to make sure I got everything right. No doubt, too, there will be mistakes in my descriptions of technical matters, though I trust they will not be major ones; as I say elsewhere, my own experience as an aviator is strictly limited.

My grateful thanks are also due to the following: The Ministry of Defence; British Airways; the Royal Air Force Museum; the Imperial War Museum; Ann Duggan; Eric Calland; Rodney S. Dalton; Squadron Leader Jack Love of RAF Coltishall; Chief Petty Officer Jack Crascall of HMS *Daedalus;* Michael Hill of HQ RAF Strike Command; Keith Ansell of RAF Support Command; Terry Fincher; Alan Reed, Picture Editor of the *Sunday Express*; Bryan Scott, Northern Picture Editor of the *Sunday Express*; and Christopher Whitehead, MoD Press Officer.

Above all, I must thank my wife Sue, the Tungsten Tulip, for the astonishing volume of work she has contributed to this book. She typed, edited, arranged, researched – *and* kept the coffee coming, yet never complained. Well, hardly ever. Without her, *Drama in the Air* would have meant much more drama in the office and could easily have ended in tears. The expensive night out at our favourite restaurant that I have promised her still won't repay the debt.

JOHN BEATTIE
North Yorkshire
November 1988

Foreword

In the 85 years since the Wright brothers first flew their biplane at Kitty Hawk, aviation has come a very long way and produced many heroes. Few readers will not have heard of Ball, McCudden and Von Richthofen (the Red Baron), Alcock and Brown, Lindbergh; and then later, of Douglas Bader, Guy Gibson, Adolf Galland and Amy Johnson. These are all household names, but of course aviation has also produced many unsung heroes and it is some of their experiences that John Beattie recounts in this book in such a readable and amusing style.

His cameos cover a wide variety of situations in which the courage, skill, tenacity and resourcefulness of those involved shine through. They focus too on many aspects of aviation, some unglamorous but all important in the contribution that they make in building up a collective understanding of the thrill, challenge, appeal and demands that flying has brought to human endeavour. I have enjoyed reading this book and I am sure that you will too.

AIR CHIEF MARSHAL SIR PATRICK HINE KCB FRAeS CBIM RAF

Commander-in-Chief United Kingdom Air Forces and Air Officer Commanding-in-Chief Strike Command

Introduction

My love affair with aeroplanes dates from the year 1945, when, as a four-year-old, I witnessed a grand Victory Parade to celebrate the end of the Second World War, an event for which I apparently insisted that my mother should dress me in the appropriately patriotic colours of red, white and blue.

I vaguely recall the lines of troops crunching past to the beat of some jaunty march. I remember seeing the spoils of war, among them a Panzer tank, I fancy, on display near the Town Hall steps. I even have a faint memory of being spectacularly sick – perhaps because of the sheer excitement of it all – on the homeward-bound tram.

What I *do* see, vividly and with undiminished clarity, even after 43 years have elapsed, is the fly-past by the Royal Air Force. In particular there was the sheer wonderment of watching a graceful Spitfire arrowing through the sky and hearing for the first time the unmistakable, grumbling growl of the Rolls-Royce Merlin engine, a sound so distinctive that, on the few occasions when it can still be heard today, I can identify the machine – Spitfire, Hurricane or Lancaster – without having to look up. As the Spitfire banked over, showing off her beautiful thoroughbred lines, I was lost. I knew in that instant that I must fly – that however strongly my friends might press the merits of engine-driving or cowpunching, I must be a pilot.

Especially I say 'thank you' to Air Chief Marshal Sir 'Paddy' Hine, Commander-in-Chief Royal Air Force Strike Command, for agreeing to write the Foreword.

Neither the passing years nor practicalities did anything to diminish that determination. I read and re-read Captain W.E. Johns's wonderful adventure books about Biggles and devoured Paul Brickhill epics like *The Dam Busters* and *Reach for the Sky*. The great airmen of the Second World War – men like Douglas Bader, Johnnie Johnson, Ginger Lacey and Bob Stanford-Tuck – became my heroes. I haunted airports and RAF stations and built the worst model aircraft in the West Riding of Yorkshire. Very soon I was an aviation bore, pestering unmercifully any relative or family friend who had happened to serve in the Air Force to tell me of his days in uniform.

Around the age of 13 – perhaps as a result of reading so many books on flying – my eyesight began to deteriorate rapidly, resulting in acute myopia. The gloomy prognostications of eye specialists did nothing to deflect me from my intent to be a pilot. Nor did the equally bleak prophecies of schoolmasters, predicting that unless my grasp of matters scientific and mathematical improved dramatically, I wouldn't get a job washing aeroplanes, let alone flying them.

Opticians and teachers were proved correct but I resolved to join up anyway. After a spell in that splendid youth organization, the Air Training Corps, I enlisted as an aircraft apprentice – or 'brat' – at No 1 School of Technical Training, Royal Air Force Halton. Alas, I quickly discoverd that working on aircraft was not the same as flying them. I was undoubtedly *in* the Royal Air Force but did not feel *of* it. My career was therefore short and undistinguished.

The RAF was pretty sporting, letting me go – 'free as an indulgence' was the splendid phrase on my discharge certificate – to become a journalist. My Air Force links were re-established when I joined the RAF Volunteer Reserve in which capacity I was able, as the old Yorkshire saying goes, to have both my bun and ha'penny – enjoying most of the benefits of Service life with few of its drawbacks.

Finally I even learned to fly, thanks to John (now Sir John) Junor, a wartime Fleet Air Arm aviator and long-serving editor of the *Sunday Express*, who agreed to finance a course of instruction so that I could write an article on how to become a pilot. On a cheerless, cold morning in 1969, after eight hours and 55 minutes of instruction, I went solo in a little Cessna 150.

The love affair had, at last, been consummated.

Following the twin paths of journalism and RAFVR service, I have come across many extraordinary stories, brought together for the first time in this book. Reading the draft manuscript I could only marvel again that such events actually happened and that I had not just invented them as rattling yarns of fiction. Truth is stranger . . .

Tom Dobney's remarkable tale of becoming a bomb pilot as a 15-year-old schoolboy is like something from the pages of *Wizard* or *Hotspur*. The iron will and unflinching gallantry of Joe Fusniak, crawling through a terrible blizzard to try to save a dying comrade, is a moving testament to the human spirit. The story Taff Holden tells of how, as a ground-based engineering officer, he took off by accident in one of the world's fastest jet fighters is the stuff that nightmares are made of.

Because of the very sporadic and haphazard way in which these chapters have been collected over the years, *Drama in the Air* emerges as something of a pot-pourri. I have, for example, included something of the work of aircraft accident investigators, those painstaking detectives who piece together the awful jigsaw puzzle of wreckage that results when drama in the air turns into tragedy on the ground. Each mystery they solve, each disaster whose cause they unravel, adds a little more to our store of knowledge. Bit by bit they help make flying – already one of the safest modes of transport – even safer.

But the greatest number of chapters chronicle the work of the airmen of the search and rescue (SAR) helicopters of the Royal Air Force and the Royal Navy – or, in one case, the gallant crew of a British Airways chopper. The deeds performed by SAR flyers often demand quite extraordinary degrees of heroism and stamina. Like lifeboatmen, they are a special breed, driven by a flinty sense of duty, a readiness to serve others and a refreshing tendency to cut the cackle and get on with the job in hand.

They are not steely-eyed demigods and they groan aloud every time some newspaper plasters its pages with yet another 'helicopter heroes' headline. They have families, mortgages, aches and pains. They usually have a well-honed, often acerbic, sense of humour. Unlike most other flyers, who rehearse for a war we all pray will never come, their war is for real, a constant war against danger and the power of the elements in which no armistice can ever be declared. They fight that war with good grace, extreme courage and a selflessness that can lead to injury or even – in the tragic instance of Dave Bullock – untimely death.

In the age of the anti-hero it has become something of a fashion for the chattering classes to smirk at words like *courage* and *selflessness*, because – one must assume – they admire the opposing qualities of cowardice and selfishness. 'Heroes are such a terrible *bore*,' a languid book editor once told me at a publisher's cocktail party in the heart of Mayfair. 'Who cares about such ghastly Action Man types?' Earlier that day I had been with a father whose two sons were still alive only because one of those despised heroes had risked his own life in mountainous seas, so I gave her a very dusty answer. Affronted, she took her smoked salmon and *Pouilly-Fumé* elsewhere.

If you think heroes are a bore – tough. It's my book. The heroes stay.

1

Taff Holden –
The Engineer's Nightmare

It is a private nightmare through which you have sweated and thrashed countless times before. Now the drug from the doctor's hypodermic is spreading through your system, unlocking the memory cells, undamming the fear of it all that is still imprisoned in your brain. The picture swims and focuses; the nightmare is pin-sharp and begins to run again like a looped tape. With it comes the terror, as real as it ever was.

Once again, you hear the wail of the engines, feel the acceleration punching you in the back, see the crazily tilted horizon in your mind's eye. Your mouth is dry, your heart is racing and your breathing is rapid and shallow. There is no escape. You are back in the cockpit again and the doctor, like a priest fighting a demon, tries to exorcise you of the ghost that has lurked there for almost four years . . .

*　　*　　*

The gremlin had been haunting Taff Holden for long enough, as cunning and stubborn a gremlin as he had ever seen in more than two decades of RAF service. Now he had had enough, the time had come to lay it by its heels once and for all.

On that sunny Friday morning, he and his crew of technicians at RAF Lyneham had the north-south runway (36) all to themselves – an empty ribbon of concrete far from the everyday bustle of the station. Only the distant whine of a circling Comet disturbed the calm of the Wiltshire countryside as Wing Commander Holden clambered up the aluminium ladder and shoehorned himself into the Lightning fighter's cramped cockpit.

The date was 22 July 1966. Four weeks had gone by, yet the 40-year-old wing commander and his team were no nearer solving the mystery of an obscure and intermittent fault in the standby electrical circuits of aircraft serial No. XM 135. Pilots reported that the gremlin showed itself only when XM 135 was surging towards take-off. Taff Holden – a Scot despite his nickname – was determined to see for himself.

He was not a pilot but an engineer, Commanding Officer of No. 33 Maintenance Unit. Even so, his intention was to recreate as authentically as possible the conditions under which the malfunction manifested itself. He would do a series of high-speed ground runs, just as though the aircraft were dashing forward for take-off. Fifty or so yards should do it. After that he could shut the throttles and brake to a standstill, long before he approached anything like V2, the point at which the pilot pulls back on the control column to take off.

Early in his RAF career he had completed primary flying training in a Tiger Moth at Queen's University Air Squadron, Belfast. His last flight had been in an amiable Chipmunk trainer in 1957, but these light planes bore as much resemblance to the 1,500-mile-an-hour Lightning F1 as a moped does to a Formula One car racing. So it was with respectful caution that Holden sat in the cockpit as civilian technicians from his workshops started up the twin Avons that made this one of the fastest and most powerful aircraft in the world.

He took a quick glance round the plumber's muddle of switches and dials. The myriad instruments gazed back like a crowd of strangers' faces – no wonder most Lightning 'jockeys' were little more than boys, young enough to have the reflexes to cope with such complexity. It all seemed a far cry from the absurd simplicity of the Tiger Moth . . .

Only a few controls need concern him: the rev-counter – methodically he distinguished it from its neighbours; the twin throttle levers beside his left thigh; and the brake lever, curiously similar to that on the handlebars of a bicycle, clamped to the handgrip of the control column; those – and the 'doll's eye' indicator that was giving all the trouble. This kept a watch on the functions of the electrical circuits and, according to pilots, had been coming on when it shouldn't. Its name described it perfectly – a round 'bubble' that flicked open like the eye of a child's doll when the standby circuits cut in after a failure of the mains. Keeping an eye on the doll's eye was why he was there.

The noise of the engines beat fiercely in his ears, louder than he had expected, for the perspex cockpit canopy had been removed to make room for the festoons of wiring and test equipment.

'Stand clear!' he called to the small knot of technicians. 'I'm off.' They backed away as he opened the throttle. The mighty engines howled to a battering crescendo; the aircraft, held only by its brakes, juddered and shook as it fought to free itself.

Holden released the brakes. The 55-foot-long fighter bounded forward like a greyhound from a trap. Dead on cue the 'doll's eye' flickered open. With a grunt of satisfaction the Scotsman closed the throttles and braked to a standstill. He scribbled quick notes on the piece of paper he had brought with him, jammed it on top of the instrument panel near the gunsight and opened up again. Once more the Lightning surged forward, this time for about 60 yards, and squealed to a halt. More notes – then another brief dash.

Now for the fourth run. It was the same procedures as before. Hold her on the brakes until the engines gave 95 per cent power, then let go of the brake lever. This time things went horribly awry . . .

A booming explosion shivered the airframe at the very instant he released the brakes. Crackling tongues of flames shot out of the twin tail pipes and XM 135 slammed forward under the brute force of 13 tons of thrust. The seat seemed to be trying to tear through his spine.

19

In shock, he tried tugging back on the throttle levers. They were locked, immovable; he couldn't kill the engines! Precious seconds ticked away as the fighter hurtled down the runway. The awful realization of what he had done struck home. By shoving the throttles too far forward, he had engaged the afterburners, designed to give pilots the punching acceleration they need for combat.

Once reheat was locked in, there was no throttling back – not without depressing two special keys that were tucked down the back of the throttle box. The brakes were useless to check that savage power.

Holden's untrained fingers scrabbled frantically. 'Luckily a technician had shown me the keys only a couple of days before,' he recalled. 'So at least I had some idea where to put my hand. But by now the speed was approaching 100 knots and suddenly a new danger made me forget everything.'

A mere 500 yards ahead an enormous fuel bowser towing a tanker trailer began to grind lazily across the runway, directly in the path of the rocketing fighter. Thousands of gallons of jet fuel swilled about in the two containers, ready-made ingredients for a major disaster.

Holden stamped desperately at the right rudder pedal, trying to steer round the back of the hazard. But there was little effect. Under the brutal spur of reheat the Lightning was arrowing along in a dead straight line. Mesmerized, the sweating wing commander watched the blue and yellow vehicle grow bigger until it seemed to fill the whole world. Then somehow it was flashing past his port wingtip, bumbling unconcernedly about its business. Its driver had not even seen the runaway aircraft; did not realize how close he had come to cremation.

Back down the runway, Holden's second-in-command, Squadron Leader Frank Seal, and the handful of technicians had witnessed the extraordinary sequence of events in disbelief and horror. At last, one found his voice. 'Dear God,' he whispered. It was more of a prayer than blasphemy. Seal leapt for his Land Rover and raced off down the perimeter track to raise the alarm.

Now the Lightning was nearing lift-off speed, straining upwards, trying to snatch her spinning wheels from the tarmac. Grimly Holden kept the stick forward, fighting the buoyancy as he jammed his hand behind the throttle box again, groping for those bloody keys. Even as his fingers found them, fate placed another cruel burden on his shoulders. He cursed and snatched his hand back on to the control column as he was propelled helplessly towards the latest peril.

Another shape was crossing in front of him . . . a Transport Command Comet nearing the end of her take-off run on the other runway. The high tailplane slid across his field of vision and vanished out of the corner of his right eye. A major disaster had been averted by scant yards.

This last danger had robbed him of the pitifully few seconds that might have given him the chance of stopping in time. Now only 500 of the 6,000 feet of runway remained. He hadn't a hope in hell. Just beyond the boundary fence was the village of Bradenstoke; Holden thought of the appalling carnage that would result as he scythed into the houses in the heart of an enormous spreading fireball.

There could be only one way. He eased back on the control column. The runway slanted down and back at incredible speed. The Lightning's gaping snout angled upwards as the polished silver shape launched itself, thrusting for the blue sky.

The rate of climb was phenomenal. Even in a steep climb a Lightning in reheat will break the sound barrier. Left to her own devices, Holden knew, XM 135 would surge higher and higher until the air of the upper atmosphere was too thin to support the stubby, swept-back wings. Then she would simply fall out of the sky.

Once more he plunged his hand down the left-hand side of his seat. With a sigh of relief he found the two keys – like small piano ivories – depressed them, and was able to ease the throttles back. The banshee howl of the engines was instantly muted. Slowly the distant hazy horizon slid back into view.

Like a man trying to recall some long-forgotten lesson, he pressed the left rudder pedal and tilted the control column in the same direction. The XM 135 dipped her port wing and

21

wobbled round. It was an unsteady turn but one that would keep her within sight of the airfield.

'She must have been perfectly trimmed because she flew straight and level like a dream,' Holden told me. 'As I cruised along the edge of the airfield at 1,500 feet I had a few moments to think; to take stock. Frankly, my thoughts did nothing to cheer me up.

'I had no cockpit canopy, no radio, no experience on jets, no means of escape and almost no hope. I was strapped into an ejector seat, but couldn't fire it because its safety pins were in place. And unless the seat left with me, I had no parachute.

'I could recognize only a few instruments and controls . . . for example, I hadn't a clue where the flap lever was. And without flaps to slow and stabilize me I would have to make a high-speed landing. Always supposing I got as far as that without killing myself.'

His eyes darted around the winking galaxy of instruments, identifying with painful slowness those he now needed most urgently – airspeed indicator, altimeter, fuel gauge, turn-and-bank indicator and artificial horizon. Then, with a start, he remembered he was cruising in the thick of the landing circuit of one of the RAF's busiest airfields. Frantically he swivelled his head, searching for the threatening bulk of the Comets and Britannias he knew to be taking off and landing.

As slowly as he dared – but not too slowly for he was terrified of stalling – he made a complete circuit of the airfield in the hope that the control tower would realize what had gone wrong. He need not have worried on that score – Squadron Leader Seal had already raised the alarm and the ether was busy with emergency calls warning the big transport planes off. Fifteen hundred feet below the fighter a cavalcade of fire-tenders and ambulances raced down the runway.

Holden watched their toy-like progress numbly. Without conscious bidding he found that vivid fragments of his boyhood in Scotland were racing through his brain. He was back to the day when, as a youngster learning to swim, he had almost drowned. *Might as well have died then. What a pointless waste to have come all this way just for this.*

22

A deep melancholy gripped him. He would die, of that he was certain. At least he would go quickly – either torn to shreds in the initial impact or instantly snuffed out by the burst of exploding fuel. What really hurt was the thought that he would never again see Jill, his wife, or their two daughters, Shirley (14) and Wendy (10). Or his son, two-year-old Nigel of whom he was so proud.

By now he was over the south-west side of the airfield, turning in for the 7,800-foot main runway – 07. He throttled back and began his fumbling, uncertain descent. Never in his life had he felt so inadequate, so hopeless. The over-sensitive controls, the surging power, his meagre stock of knowledge, all combined to make him feel totally useless.

Bloody fool! He cursed himself savagely. What a way to go, smeared out of existence in a spreading ball of flame. All because he, a senior engineering officer who should have known better, had been idiotically careless with a piece of machinery. Then the anger drained away. There was no time for it – only for concentrating every fibre on flying for his life as the wings rocked in over the runway threshold.

It was all wrong from the start. The height was wrong. The speed was wrong. The direction was wrong. The landing could be nothing but sheer catastrophe. His breath rasped harshly in his throat as he shoved the throttles open and went round again, off on another madcap circuit of Lyneham. The slipstream buffeted into the open cockpit, yet his pencilled notes still lay undisturbed near the gunsight. 'Damned good streamlining,' he mused inconsequentially.

As he circled the airbase the disciplined training of 23 years' RAF service came to the fore. He used the time wisely, experimenting with different throttle settings and gentle control movements to get the 'feel' of the aircraft.

Yet his second attempt at landing was even worse than the first. Down . . . down . . . down . . . left a bit . . . the muscles of his arms and legs kept knotting with tension as he strove to keep XM 135 aimed towards the narrow lifeline of concrete that gradually changed shape from two parallel lines to an ever-broadening triangle.

Quite suddenly it simply vanished.

Hell! Holden threw the throttles forward, knowing death was only seconds away. Now he was actually *below* the level of the runway, racing across a shallow valley towards the tree-lined escarpment upon whose summit the airfield was built.

Slowly, too damned slowly, the nose came up as the Lightning roared towards the woods. For a wild moment he even considered re-engaging reheat to climb clear, but then the trees were slipping away scant feet below as the aircraft hurdled the ridge like a hunter tackling a five-barred gate. The startled watchers, waiting beside the runway for the rumble of an explosion and pall of black smoke, ducked instinctively as the rocking wings flashed over their heads.

Another chance missed. Holden swore bleakly. To put her down now would mean overshooting the runway and ploughing into Lyneham village, turning it into a charnel house. If, however, he were to come in from the opposite direction – on Runway 25 – he would have two advantages. First, he would be landing up a slight incline to help him slow down. And second, if he did overshoot he would crash over the escarpment, almost certainly incinerating himself but at least endangering no one else. It was a grim prospect, but there was no other choice.

He flew another complete circuit, turning over the village and making a pass down the runway in the 'wrong' direction to warn those on the ground of his intentions. Back round again and he was making a long, flat approach across the roofs, easing down towards the 150-foot-wide strip. This time he felt a stab of hope. Everything seemed much better – the angle, the speed, the height. For the first time since take-off he dared to contemplate the chance of getting down in one piece and seeing his family again.

Not that his problems were over. Far from it. Lightnings, they say, don't land – they suffer a controlled crash. The actual touchdown speed of a fighter is governed by the weight of fuel it carries – Holden did not know the equation. He would have to land without flaps; that meant he would have to come in fast in order not to stall. And he had never done a touchdown in an aircraft with a nose wheel, an entirely different landing technique from his own strictly limited experience on light aircraft with tail wheels.

He opened the throttles slightly as he whistled over the village streets. Immediately XM 135 felt more stable, less mushy. The speed was around 180 miles an hour. The runway hurtled towards him at a frightening velocity, looking depressingly short. Surely he would over-run it and die in a funeral pyre of his own making.

Two hundred feet . . . 100 . . . 50. The boundary fence flashed past. The nose lifted as he flared out and eased the throttles back. She sank. There was a barely perceptible jar as the high-pressure tyres kissed smoke from the concrete.

Incredibly, it was almost a copy-book landing. Only one thing marred it. From behind and below there was a faint clunk which the elated wing commander could not identify. He crawled the throttles back and pushed the stick forward to force the nose wheel on to the runway, yanking the brake-parachute release to slow his headlong dash. Briefly the toughened 'chute fluttered out behind the tail, then billowed away uselessly. Later he discovered the clunk had been the rubber tail-bumper striking the ground. The impact had somehow severed the parachute cable, robbing him of this vital lifeline.

At the time, though, Holden knew none of this. All he did know was that he was still racketing along at a fearsome speed. He squeezed with all his might on the brake lever and felt his headlong dash begin to check as the discs bit hard. At this speed he was burning them out fast. If only the fibre pads – now blazing and smoking with friction – would hold out a little longer before melting or disintegrating . . .

She was juddering and jolting like a mad thing, her brakes screaming with the strain, only a few hundred yards to go before she dashed herself into extinction among the trees. A wailing, flashing motorcade of rescue vehicles, racing flat out, closed on the bucking fighter.

Just 300 feet from the end of the concrete the Lightning stopped. Clouds of smoke, acrid with the stench of burning rubber, caught her up and drifted by. Without knowing what he was doing, the shaken wing commander released the brakes and began taxiing down the perimeter track towards the control tower.

Squadron Leader Seal sprinted across the grass and flagged him down. 'Come on, sir,' he shouted. 'Get out. You've gone far enough.'

Holden nodded wearily and shut down the engines. In a deafening silence he looked at his watch. The nightmare had lasted just 12 minutes.

*　　　*　　　*

An hour later he walked through the front door of his married quarters. Upstairs Jill Holden was changing for the garden party they were due to attend that afternoon. Unaware of the drama that had been enacted above her, she looked at her husband with curiosity as he sat wearily on the bed and rested his head on his hands.

'What's wrong, Taff?' she asked.

That was the moment the tension and mental strain caught up with him.

'I just broke down,' he said. 'It was a terribly emotional moment . . . to see Jill again after being convinced I never would. I told her all about what had happened and, after a bit, felt all right. So we went off to the garden party.

'Much later, a doctor told me that instead of drinking tea I should have gone to the Mess and polished off a bottle of whisky. Getting drunk would have drained my system of the trauma of it all. As it was it stayed with me for a long time afterwards.'

It stayed with him through the court of inquiry. Through the subsequent 'rocket' – and the pat on the back for landing XM 135 in one piece. Through two nervous breakdowns. Not until four years after that incredible 12 minutes of horror did he walk out of its shadow. To do it he had to submit to the doctor's drugs that made him fly over and over again until the nightmare was expunged from his mind.

Fifteen years after that traumatic Friday morning, Wing Commander W.V. Holden MBE retired from the Royal Air

Force, something of a celebrity, and went to live in rural Buckinghamshire. The aircraft that shared his brief moment of notoriety remains carefully preserved by the Imperial War Museum at Duxford Airfield, Cambridgeshire.

His logbook contains the following entry: 'July 22, 1966 – Lightning F1 No. XM 135. Inadvertent flight – 12 minutes.'

It was his last entry . . . until his 60th birthday on 7 November 1986, when – 20 years later – he climbed into a Cessna light plane with an instructor and took off from Halton airfield, a few miles from his home, for a one-hour trial flight.

'It was something I had to do, to take control of an aircraft for the last time,' he explained. 'I needed to get it out of my system; to finally rid myself of the fear of flying.'

Sixty minutes later, Taff Holden stepped out of the tiny monoplane, smiling with pleasure. He had enjoyed the flight through the wintry sunshine above the rolling Chiltern Hills.

Best of all, he knew that an old ghost had finally been laid to rest.

2

Jim Clark –
The Winchman's Narrow
Escape

Perched precariously 1,000 feet up a near-sheer mountainside, Jim Clark chanced an unhappy look downwards at the
void that lay between him and a bone-crunching death on
the jumble of boulders nearly a quarter of a mile below. He
quickly wished he hadn't. Heights had always given him the
flutters; the sheer immensity of this one caused his heart to
race with alarm.

His clothing was wildly inappropriate for scrabbling about
vertical rockfaces in the Scottish Isles – a sweaty immersion
suit, crash helmet and a clumsy pair of rubber boots. He
pressed his cheek closer to the warm rock, wriggling his toes
for a firmer grip. *Christ, Jim lad, you've really done it this
time*, he told himself. *Rock-climbing in a pair of wellies*.

The day had got off to an inauspicious enough start – a curt
note in the post from Elgin Sheriff's Court fining him £20 for
a minor motoring offence to which he had pleaded guilty by
letter.

Then there had been a busy shift at RAF Lossiemouth
beside the Moray Firth – a whole series of seemingly endless exercises, practice flying for his role as a Whirlwind
helicopter winchman with 'D' Flight, No 202 Squadron.
After twenty years in the Royal Air Force, which had
brought him to warrant officer rank at the pinnacle of
the NCO pyramid, No X4167956 Master Signaller James

Frood Clark still loved flying.

But there were occasions when it could be too much of a good thing, especially when it placed him in a position where only inexpert experimenting with unfamiliar toe and finger holds kept him from a particularly messy and spectacular demise.

It was, he decided, turning out to be one of those days.

*   *   *

In fact, it had been one of those glorious summer days, hot and still with gin-clear skies, that show off the Scottish Highlands at their breathtaking best . . . a day to lose yourself in a secluded glen and sit with a picnic hamper beside a chattering burn.

On that Thursday evening – 17 July 1975 – RAF Lossiemouth was quiet, the day's flying ended. The Air Force's Jaguar strike aircraft and the Royal Navy's rumbling, grumbling anti-submarine Gannets were hangared for the night. A lark tumbled exultantly beneath blue skies, its sweet song the only sound on the vast, empty airfield. The sun was beating a retreat across the Moray Firth, trailing lengthening coat-tails of shadows in its wake. A warm breeze, the merest zephyr, barely stirred the grass.

For the duty crew in 'D' Flight's headquarters, their evening meal over, it was a time for loafing round the crewroom, reading, smoking, catching up on official bumf or playing uckers, the British serviceman's version of ludo, a rather more vicious variety than the drawing-room one.

The 7.30 p.m. call from the duty officer at the Northern Rescue Coordination Centre at Pitreavie Castle near Edinburgh, was – like all such calls – brief and to the point. There had been a climbing accident in the Cuillins, the precipitous mountain range on the south of the Isle of Skye. A mountaineer had fallen on the 1,300-foot peak called Sron na Ciche. His safety rope had saved him from death, but he was badly injured and in urgent need of medical care. Over to 'D' Flight.

The duty crew unfolded the Ordnance Survey map of Skye and began tracing the grid reference they had been given. They were three in number: the captain, Flight Lieutenant Geoff Leeming; navigator Flight Lieutenant Bill Gault; and winchman Jim Clark.

The master signaller whistled as his finger found the spot on the map. 'Bloody hell,' he said, 'just take a look at that little lot.'

Before metrication, the Ordnance Survey's brown contour lines showed each height difference of 50 feet. Sron na Ciche's peak was ringed by almost solid brown, denoting a precipitous slope. It was a thoughtful trio that made its way out of the dispersal hut into that glorious summer's evening.

The Gnome gas turbine of the canary yellow rescue machine stirred itself and whined into life as they carried out their pre-take-off checks. Leeming opened the throttle, the 53-foot main rotor flexed, took the strain and hoisted 3½ tons of aircraft into the evening sky.

The trip across the narrow neck of Scotland above the mountains and lochs of Inverness-shire was breathtakingly beautiful but uneventful. Leeming in the pilot's seat, Gault beside him on his left and Clark, sitting in the doorway with his feet dangling in space, all had time to savour the panorama unfolding beneath them.

An hour after take-off they were picking their way through the soaring peaks of the Cuillins. The sinking sun had turned the mountains into a dappled patchwork of light and shade – rockfaces etched in golden sunlight, deep boulder-strewn corries almost lost in inky shadows.

Already the transit across the Highlands from east to west had made deep inroads into the Whirlwind's fuel capacity. Leeming prudently elected to refuel before beginning the search for the injured man. There was little point in finding him, only to break off in order to fill emptying tanks. He headed a mile or so to the west, to Glenbrittle, where the RAF maintained an emergency fuel dump. There police officers and members of the Skye Mountain Rescue Team had gathered in the field used as a landing ground.

As Clark supervised the rolling out of 45-gallon drums and the hand-pumping of fuel into the aircraft, Geoff Leeming was receiving an update on the situation. When the first alert had come, Gerry Ackroyd, leader of the mountain rescue team, had begun climbing Sron na Ciche, leaving instructions for the rest of the team to follow when they had assembled. Already he was close to the 18-inch ledge on which the injured man was lying and, via a borrowed police two-way radio, was painting a word picture of the scene.

The climber, George Yeomans, from County Durham, had broken his wrist and was suffering from serious head injuries. His two fellow climbers were roped to the face 15 feet above him – 1,000 feet up from the floor of the corrie. Could the helicopter ferry extra ropes to the 1,300-foot summit in case it became necessary to lower him to safety?

'Tell him we'll take the ropes up to the top,' Leeming told the policeman who had relayed the message. 'Then we'll go and have a look. If we can't do anything we'll put some of the mountain rescue boys on the summit so they can climb down to him. It'll be a damn sight faster than them hoofing it up from here.'

Heavy with replenished fuel tanks, her cabin loaded with drums of ropes, the Whirlwind took off and turned towards the menacing bulk of Sron na Ciche. Just finding the spot was a headache, for every valley, corrie, ridge and col looked bewilderingly alike. Navigator Gault carefully picked a course through the pinnacles and canyons until the mountain hoved into view. Slowly they circled it.

'There!' Geoff Leeming's voice came over the intercom as the chopper clattered into a corrie, a deep bowl-like depression almost surrounded by encircling mountains. It was like flying through the open jaws of a horseshoe.

The face to which the climbers clung was on the helicopter's right and lit by brilliant sunshine, a near-vertical wall of basalt reaching up from the gloomy corrie floor to a height of 1,300 feet. About 300 feet below the summit the mountaineers hung from a flimsy web of safety ropes. In the doorway on the helicopter's starboard side Jim Clark's stomach lurched with apprehension as he contemplated the prospect of being winched down on the seemingly smooth rockface.

'Someone's got to be kidding,' he said in disbelief. 'It's bloody impossible.'

'Shouldn't have joined if you can't take a joke,' Leeming replied. 'Now we know where they are we'll go up top and dump the ropes – then come back for another look.'

Though Sron na Ciche reaches 1,300 feet above the ground, the summit is actually 2,500 feet above sea level, way beyond the Whirlwind's normal operating height. Very slowly and reluctantly she clawed for altitude until at last she cleared the brink of the mountain top. On the other side was an apparently flat area – almost a plateau – an ideal place to dump the ropes for the mountain rescue boys.

As they hovered a few feet above it Clark rolled the drums containing the ropes out through the open door, watching first with surprise, then with mortification, as they bounced and began to roll away with ever-increasing speed. The 'plateau' had been an optical illusion – not flat ground after all, but a relatively steep slope. The precipitous terrain, with no horizon against which the pilot could align his machine, had fooled them all. They groaned in frustration as the ropes bounced downhill for almost half a mile before fetching up in a clump of boulders.

Definitely one of those days . . .

Heat as well as height knocks the edge off any helicopter's performance – and it had been a very hot day. The sun-soaked rocks of the Cuillins were still radiating heat. That, combined with altitude, had meant the Whirlwind had to gasp for every foot on the run to the summit. It quickly became obvious that she was carrying far too much weight for the prolonged hover demanded during winching; even at full throttle she would slowly but steadily lose altitude. So Leeming circled for several minutes, jettisoning fuel from the tanks beneath the cabin floor until only 450 pounds of kerosene remained. Because fuel gauges are notoriously inaccurate – often tending to over-read – RAF regulations demanded that a Whirlwind must fly no more when the dial showed 150 pounds of fuel remaining. Thus the only *known* fuel that Leeming had was 300 pounds, sufficient for perhaps 20 minutes at full throttle in the hover.

With this slender margin swilling in his tanks the pilot once more flew out over the void and circled back towards the group of men on the precipice. As he did so, Bill Gault left the second pilot's seat and clambered down the bulkhead behind the flight deck into the aftercabin where Jim Clark was preparing himself. Clark had already clipped his safety harness and a Neil Robertson folding stretcher to the winch hook. Attached to his lifejacket was a special search and rescue beacon (SARBE). As well as emitting a constant signal to enable an aircraft to home in on him, it also incorporated a simple two-way radio permitting him some degree of communication with Geoff Leeming.

Gault knelt in the doorway beside Clark and disconnected the winchman's helmet jack-plug from the aircraft intercom system. Gault's job was vital. During winching, the pilot would rely on him totally to describe what was happening at the end of the winch wire, out of sight behind and below.

Like a man preparing to dive into a deep pool, Jim Clark took a deep breath as the navigator rocked the winch switch to swing him out of the door and begin lowering. Turning gently in the rotor's downwash he gazed down the dizzy reaches of the mountainside and, in no time at all, decided he was wasting his time. He didn't stand even the slimmest chance of getting anywhere near the injured man or Gerry Ackroyd, the mountain rescue leader, who had now reached him. About 15 feet above them were George Yeomans's two companions, still roped to the rock with their safety lines.

Leeming was hovering with great skill, the starboard flank of his machine parallel with the rockface, the tips of his rotor blades whirling only feet from the mountain. The rule book says a pilot must allow half the rotor span as clearance; Leeming had chucked away the rule book, but still he could not get close enough. Clark hung helplessly below the fuse-lage. The rock was 25 feet away. It might just as well have been 25 miles. He looked up at Gault and spread his arms in an eloquent, almost Gallic, shrug that was as plain as the spoken word.

Leeming steered away from the wall for a brief conference with his navigator. Clark, of course, was not privy to it, since his link to the intercom had been broken, but he soon got the drift of the plan when Gault began to pantomime from the doorway.

The idea was simple: the aircraft would go lower and, using a longer wire, Gault would try to land him on a slightly prominent breast of rock some 25 feet below the ledge. Clark nodded; he had got it. As he descended he craned his head upwards. Like an angler boasting of a whopping catch, his arms were outstretched – indicating to Gault the gap between rotor blades and mountain. When he was finally in line with the rock breast, the winchman noted grimly that his hands were only 30 inches apart!

If the pilot so much as hiccoughed, the blades would touch the mountain to be instantly flayed into splinters. As night follows day, the Whirlwind would fall out of the sky and the three RAF men would die.

Through the whirling disc of the blades Clark could see another potential hazard – just a few feet up were Yeomans's white-faced friends. For them the clamour of the engine and the sight of the blades clopping round just beneath their feet must have been awesome.

For God's sake don't move, he willed them.

If you do, you're mincemeat and we're dead. And don't dislodge any stones for Christ's sake.

He looked around. Certainly he was now far closer to the face of the mountain, but the gap was still 15 feet. He began swinging himself on the end of the wire, twisting and jerking his body like some escape artist laden with chains. Gault twigged what he was doing right away and leaned out of the door to grab the wire. Alternately pushing and pulling on it, he set up an ever-increasing pendulum effect, while Leeming made constant, delicate control movements to iron out the sympathetic lurches of the helicopter.

Clark was swinging wildly now, each time arcing closer to the rock and reaching out for the spot he had decided was the best place to get a grip – a small anvil of basalt. His world had become a crazy kaleidoscope of sunshine and shadow, rock

34

and sky, all whirling around at a speed that made him giddy. The mountain raced towards him and he jammed his feet out in front to take the impact. They just touched. With a grunt he kicked off, curving back over the chasm. Next time he hit harder, bending his knees and shoving off with all his might. He whirled out into space – and then swung back towards Sron na Ciche, his hands outstretched for the target.

He hit with a force that momentarily winded him, flung his left arm round the rock and steadied himself with his right hand as though putting a neck-lock on a wrestling opponent. The rubber boots of his immersion suit scrabbled for a toe hold on the smooth surface, his sweaty face rasped painfully against the rock and his lungs were labouring to suck in air. But he had made it.

Gradually he regained his breath. After an age he found a minute foothold and was able to inch himself slightly higher to get a better grip on his hunk of rock. He glanced up and grinned with a confidence he was far from feeling at the concerned face of Gerry Ackroyd peering at him from the ledge 25 feet above.

In that moment Jim Clark found himself making what turned out to be an extraordinarily gallant decision. If he stayed linked to the winch the trailing wire would hamper his climb. Then there was the burden of the 14-pound lead weight fixed to the top of the hook to ensure that the apparatus hung down as straight as a plumbline. Furthermore, every second he spent on the mountain meant Geoff Leeming having to fly to the finest tolerances, holding his craft steady at high throttle settings that would drink fuel at a furious rate.

He unhooked himself. The winch wire danced free and swung beneath the Whirlwind's wheels. Bill Gault's voice went up an octave in the pilot's headset: 'Bloody hell, he's fallen off!' Then a sigh of relief and: 'No hang on, he's unhooked himself.'

Leeming, realizing that his crewman had given him the chance to move away from the threatening rockface and circle at a more economical throttle setting, observed grimly: 'I just hope he likes rock-climbing.'

About then, Clark, who had never been mountaineering before, was deciding that of all the pastimes he could think of, rock-climbing would win his personal award for the most fatuous. For as long as he could recall, heights had made him extremely uncomfortable. Not, oddly enough, when he was flying – that was somehow different. But to be in a high place always made his head swim slightly. Apprehensively he looked down and took a deep gulp. It was like leaning over the roof of a New York skyscraper; nothing but air between him and the ground.

The familiar roar of the Whirlwind had dwindled as Leeming described far-away circles to conserve fuel. Now all Jim Clark could hear was the rasping of his own breath and the thud of his heart. He felt horribly alone – *was* alone, for no one in the world could help him now. One slip and he was dead. With painstaking care he began to climb, trying not to look down at the drop as he shoved the folded stretcher up the rock ahead of him.

Jam your feet in that fissure . . . reach up with the left hand and feel around . . . ah, there's a grip . . . now rest the stretcher against your chest and ease your right hand on to that little ridge . . . feel for another toe hold . . . keep looking UP! Concentrate, man, concentrate . . .

Inch by inch he crawled up the nightmarish wall, only half-hearing the shouts of encouragement and advice from the climbers above. Sweat rolled down inside his rubber suit, soaking the woollen long-johns inside. No sane mountaineer would have tackled the climb without proper boots, pitons and ropes. Yet there was Clark attempting it dressed up like the Michelin man. He hitched himself another 6 inches towards the ridge.

A century or so later he managed to hook his right hand over the ledge. With a supreme effort he raised his chin to the same level and found himself looking into Gerry Ackroyd's concerned face. The mountain rescue leader's strong hands gripped him beneath the armpits and hauled him on to the ledge. 'That was quite some climb,' he said. Clark, gasping like a stranded fish on the narrow stone parapet, could only nod.

'Reaching the ledge was a tremendous moment,' Clark told me after he had retired from the RAF and was flying as a winchman with British Airways helicopters. 'Throughout the climb I'd had the constant thought that if I made a mistake I could kiss goodbye to everything. It concentrated the mind wonderfully.

'I was apprehensive, but curiously enough not particularly scared. That came two or three days later when I found myself waking up in a sweat during the wee small hours thinking "What the hell was I doing there?" During the climb itself, I suppose I was too busy for fear.'

The RAF man crawled along the ledge and bent over Yeomans. Despite his broken wrist, an ugly wound on his right temple and painful bruising of the torso where his rope had jerked him up short, he was still conscious. He even managed a weak smile when Clark promised him he would soon be in hospital.

The two other climbers made their way down to the ledge to help strap their companion into the stretcher. Like Ackroyd, they were on safety lines; Clark, kneeling with his toes hanging out over space, was only too conscious that there was nothing to secure him from the void behind. It made him feel horribly vulnerable.

He got the climbers to roll the injured man on to his side, facing the rock. He unfolded the stretcher and slid it into position, then Yeomans was allowed to sink on to it on his back. Finally he was securely trussed in and Clark was able to turn his mind to the problem which had been nagging him ever since his lunatic trapeze act on the end of the winch wire.

How to get back on the hook.

His flesh crawled at the prospect of trying to climb back down to his original perch. He doubted he could manage it on his own, let alone while manhandling a loaded stretcher. That, he reckoned, would be the quick way to get off the mountain – the few seconds it would take two of them to fall 1,000 feet.

And yet he already had proof positive that it was impossible for the helicopter to get close enough to winch directly from the ledge on which he was perched. There

was, however, one way that might work . . . He unclipped
the SARBE from his Mae West (lifejacket) and spoke into
the mouthpiece, explaining what he had in mind. There was
a delay of several minutes before Leeming's voice crackled
over the air: 'OK, Jim – we've done that and we're ready to
give it a whirl. Stand by, we're coming in now.'

Silhouetted against the dazzling gold of a spectacular sun-
set, the Whirlwind thundered towards the mountain, filling
the black corrie with echoes. The winch wire was lowered
to its maximum reach of 60 feet. Knotted to the hook and
dancing in the downwash was Clark's brainchild . . . more
than 100 feet of half-inch nylon rope. Lashed to the end was
a karabiner, a stout metal fastening of the type employed by
mountaineers for anchoring themselves. He would use this to
attach himself and the stretcher to the rope.

He explained to Ackroyd and the two other climbers: 'The
extension rope has given us around 180 feet to play with.
That means the pilot can hover much higher and the guy in
the doorway doesn't have to swing the wire so far. Even so,
it'll still be at something of an angle so once we lift off there'll
be a hell of a swing away from the ledge, then we'll seesaw
back and hit the rock if we're not careful.

'Once I'm on the hook with the stretcher, I want you to
give me one end of a rope and hang on to the other end
yourself. When we've been lifted off, take the weight and
ease us out gently until we're hanging straight down. Then
I'll let go and you can haul your rope back in. OK?'

They nodded. It all sounded straightforward enough, they
supposed.

The line on the winch hook trailed towards the ledge.
Hanging out into space at the utmost stretch of their safety
lines the climbers tried to grab it but, tantalizingly, it snaked
just out of reach. Bill Gault, however, had anticipated this
problem. Close to the end of the rope he had lashed a spare
lifejacket. Without it the line would have curled and kinked
in mid-air; with it there was just enough weight for him to get
it swinging in the same pendulum motion as before.

The rope end flicked closer. There was a shout from one
of the climbers. 'Got the bugger!' Two minutes later Clark's

harness and the lifting straps of the stretcher were clipped to the karabiner. The winchman took a deep breath: 'Right, let's see if this lash-up works.' He waved to the helicopter high above him, heard the engine note change and felt his boots slowly lift off the ledge.

'Pay it out,' he yelled to the climbers. 'Easy does it.' It worked like a charm. As soon as Clark could see he was hanging from a straight line he let the climbers' rope go and waved farewell. The three men, laughing and cheering, waved back with enthusiasm and the Whirlwind wheeled away from the rock wall. Shifting perspectives gave him a fresh angle from which to view the staggering drop into the twilit corrie. Despite the suffocating heat inside his rubber suit he felt himself shiver. There was a momentary deliquescence deep in his bowels as he visualized the fall that would have resulted if he had slipped from the rockface.

The dying rays of the sun transmuted Sron na Ciche's summit into pure gold as the helicopter descended towards the corrie floor. The ride was oddly soft and springy, thanks to the elasticity of the nylon rope. It was quiet too – with the chopper hovering nearly 200 feet above his head the engine noise was muted to a distant growl. Clark smiled reassurance at the man he had rescued. 'I hope you're not frightened of heights, mate. Because if you are, don't look over your shoulder.'

Five minutes later his feet touched ground – beautiful, level, safe Scottish turf. He quickly unclipped his harness from the karabiner, unhitched the stretcher and loosed the extension rope from the hook. Coiling it over his shoulder, he attached himself and the stretcher to the winch cable and was lifted smoothly towards the cabin door. A grinning Bill Gault swung them inboard. By now, the fuel gauge was indicating a reserve way below the permitted minimum of 150 pounds; theoretically, at least, the tanks could already be bone dry. So they had to refuel once more at Glenbrittle before continuing to Broadford hospital, 20 miles due east, where the casualty department had been alerted to the imminent arrival of George Yeomans. Stretcher-bearers and nurses waited by the helipad in the grounds.

The operation had been 'D' Flight's one-thousandth rescue mission. Undoubtedly it was its most spectacular. Months later Jim Clark was awarded the Air Force Cross to go with the Air Force Medal he had won two years earlier as a flight sergeant – making him one of the select few in the RAF entitled to the initials AFC, AFM after his name. The citation for the former tells of his 'skill, courage and selfless determination to succeed.'

But gongs from the Queen were the farthest thing from his mind when he stood at the reception desk of the hospital, watching George Yeomans being wheeled away on a trolley. He gave the youngster an encouraging thumbs-up, then turned as a nurse called him: 'Mr Clark? A call for you or any member of your crew.' She proffered the telephone.

It was the coastguard duty officer at Stornaway. 'Lossiemouth told us where to find you.' he said. 'We'd be grateful for your help. We've got an overdue yacht on our books and we were wondering if you could just buzz over and have a look . . .'

Clark sighed. He had known all along that it was going to be one of those days.

3

Tom Dobney – Schoolboy Pilot

I first came across Tom Dobney's remarkable saga some 10 years ago when I was the Assistant Editor of the *Sunday Express*'s Northern office in Manchester. At the time I was engaged in writing a series of articles about men and women who had managed to survive a variety of ordeals in the face of heavy odds. One concerned a wartime member of the SAS who, without food or water, had made an epic trek through the Libyan desert, evading Rommel's troops and surviving by drinking his own urine. I wanted to know what the record was for desert survival and sent to the *Express* library on the next floor for the *Guinness Book of Records*.

For the record, Norris McWhirter's splendid book was not able to furnish me with the information I was after that day. What it did do though, as on innumerable occasions before and since, was to sidetrack me gloriously and hopelessly, seducing me from the task in hand as I riffled through page after page of fascinating facts and figures. Amid the treasure trove the following entry seemed to spring at me from the printed page:

The youngest age at which anyone has ever qualified as a military pilot is 15 years 5 months in the case of Sergeant Thomas Dobney (born 6 May 1926) of the RAF.

I blinked. Provided the story was 'new' (i.e. had not been reported by any of the Fleet Street papers) I had something which had all the makings of a first-class feature article, even though 30 years had elapsed since the end of the war. For the time being my SAS man was forgotten while I unleashed the librarians on 75 million cuttings from the *Express* papers and their Fleet Street rivals. While they searched, I rang the London office library and asked the staff there to begin hunting for an envelope marked 'Dobney, Thomas'. When both libraries reported that they had drawn a blank I was delighted for that was almost certain proof that the story had never been written – that I was sitting on a hitherto-untold tale of the Second World War. With relish, I toyed with headlines – perhaps 'Classroom Pilot – A Schoolboy's War'? But could I find this intriguing Thomas Dobney so many years on?

So began a minor epic in its own right. The *Guinness Book of Records* people were unable to come up with Dobney's whereabouts, as were the Ministry of Defence, the Royal Air Force Club, the Royal Air Forces Association, the Royal British Legion or any of the half-dozen other ex-servicemen's organizations I tried. I contacted old RAF friends of my own, scoured the Royal Air Force List and rang repeatedly until I had spoken to every one of the 11 Dobneys listed in the London telephone directory. The option of poring through *every* telephone book in the land – there are about 200 – I rejected. Perhaps, if all else failed, I might try that as a final resort.

Yet even that mammoth, boring task would prove nothing. It wouldn't tell me whether Dobney had been killed during the war or had died subsequently. Nor would it help me if he was not on the telephone or, for some reason, was an ex-directory subscriber. No phone book could tell me if he had emigrated, changed his name or was serving a prison sentence. The permutations were endless.

When, two weeks later, I had exhausted all the usual journalistic tricks employed to trace people, I sat down and wrote a brief note to an old friend, Charles Worrall, then the Royal Air Force's Senior Press Officer in Whitehall, explaining my interest in the Dobney story. With it I enclosed a letter to the man himself, asking him to contact me at the *Sunday Express* office in Great Ancoats Street, Manchester. Charles wrote back to say that RAF Records at Gloucester were searching their files for the last-known address of the mysterious schoolboy pilot. All I could do was wait patiently, fervently hoping I wouldn't have to start wading through the United Kingdom's 200 phone books after all.

Soon afterwards, I went to work in the United States for a couple of months and the Dobney saga began to slip further down my list of priorities. By the time I returned to England, I had almost forgotten it. Upon my return, however, I received a call from Charles Worrall.

'We have managed to trace your boy pilot for you,' he announced proudly.

'That's wonderful, Charles,' I enthused. 'But now give me the bad news – tell me how he lives in Australia or Outer Monogolia or anywhere the paper won't cough up an airline ticket for.'

There was a chuckle on the line. 'Well, you'll have to do *some* travelling to get to his present home, old boy. Have you got a pen?'

I could hardly believe my luck when he spelled out Dobney's address. It was in a country town right in the heart of the Manchester commuter belt, less than a dozen miles from where I was sitting. I promised Worrall a double when we next met and hung up. In the Manchester phone book I found an entry for Dobney, T. and dialled the number.

No, Mr Dobney was not there at the moment; was at his office. The number? Certainly – 061–236–2112.

I looked bemusedly at the number I had scribbled down. It was my own number, the switchboard of Express Newspapers.

'What does Mr Dobney do for a living?' I asked rather light-headedly.

'He's a journalist. Works for the *Daily Express*,' came the reply.

I mumbled my thanks and replaced the receiver. Turning to the reporter who worked on the next desk, I asked if he knew anyone by the name of Dobney.

'Oh, yes, you mean Tom Dobney. Works on the *Daily Express* picture desk.' My colleague pointed across the wide editorial floor that we Sunday paper men shared with our daily colleagues. 'That's him over there, the bloke with the slide rule in his hand. He was hired when you were away in the States.'

Twenty paces was all it took, then I was beside his desk, shaking hands with the man I had been seeking for the past few months.

'My name's John Beattie,' I said. 'I've been looking for you.'

*　　　*　　　*

The first enemy guns that were ever trained on Tom Dobney opened up on a bitter, freezing January night in 1942. The two Merlin engines of his Whitley bomber were roaring flat out as, stick hard over, he steered towards a huge bank of cloud, a shadowy canopy edged with the silver glow of moonlight. But the shelter it offered seemed a million miles away.

Circling like hungry barracuda, a pair of Messerschmidt night fighters pulled in a tight turn and lined up with the lumbering Armstrong Whitworth-built machine with its curious nose-down flight attitude. Out of the darkness came pretty, sparkling lights from the Germans' winking cannon and machine guns. From the Whitley's tail turret, the rear gunner kept up a spirited defence with his four Brownings. But it was a hopelessly unequal contest. The Luftwaffe machines could fly at nearly 400 miles per hour; flat out the bomber might rumble along at 230 miles per hour. Their 20-millimetre Mauser cannon outgunned the British machine's .303 machineguns. The Messerschmidts were thoroughbred racehorses; the Whitley was a carthorse.

The outcome of the battle was virtually a foregone conclusion. If the RAF plane didn't manage to duck into the cloud she would be blasted out of the sky. Tom Dobney tried to wheedle a few more precious knots from her, but the throttles were already fully forward on maximum boost. His arms ached with the strain of heaving the heavy controls in violent evasive action and the patch of forehead that showed between his helmet and eyebrows glistened with the sheen of a muck-sweat.

The tail gunner roared warning of another attack and he slammed the controls to port. Just in time – bright rods of tracer danced past a few feet from his head and faded into the distance.

Where *was* that damned cloud? It seemed as far away as ever. His fur-booted foot kicked viciously at the right rudder pedal; his gloved hand yanked the control column. The heavy bomber, creaking in protest, lurched to starboard, nimbly sidestepping another stream of shells. In spite of himself, Dobney grinned into his oxygen mask. *If only the lads back home in Nuneaton could see him now . . .*

'Here they come again,' bawled the tail gunner with deafening force. Rowdy beggar, the young pilot thought as he jammed the nose down. He really would have to have words with that gunner about yelling over the intercom.

At that moment the windscreen went blank. At long, long last he had hit that wonderful, safe, all-enveloping, cloud. He settled back in his seat, feeling the knotted muscles in the small of his back unclench as the worst of the tension drained away. There was a click in his earphones, followed by the navigator's voice. 'Well done, Skipper – bloody good show.'

Sergeant Thomas Dobney, Royal Air Force, bomber captain and trustee of his own and four other men's lives, looked back on the busiest few minutes of his young life with some satisfaction. He had been tested and not found lacking. The youngest military pilot the world has ever known had just proved himself under fire.

At the age of 15.

*   *   *

Cussy Coward had started it all. He and Tom Dobney, both 14, shared the same desk in the Lower Sixth of King Edward VI's Grammar School in Nuneaton, Warwickshire, and followed the war news avidly. In that summer of 1940 they watched the progress of the Battle of Britain even more keenly than they had scanned Test Match results before war had broken out. They wanted somehow to play their part. But how? Already they had been laughed out of the local police station when they had tried to volunteer as messengers. 'Come back when your voices have broken,' the desk sergeant teased them.

On a warm afternoon in August, during the school holidays, the big idea was born. The two boys were idling in Nuneaton town centre when a colourful display in a shop window caught their eyes.

'FLY WITH THE RAF!' a poster exhorted.

Cussy grabbed Tom's arm. 'Hey,' he said, jabbing a finger towards the window. 'Bet you daren't try it.'

'You watch me,' retorted his friend and boldly pushed open the door. He felt his confidence ebb, however, as a bemedalled flight sergeant straightened up from his desk and stood towering above the youngster's 5 foot 4 inch frame.

'Come to join the Brylcreem boys have you, son?'

With a quaver in the voice he had dropped a tone, the lad answered. 'Yes please. I'd like to know how to join as a pilot.'

The airman handed over a bundle of pamphlets. 'Here, take this bumf home. It'll give you all the gen.'

Tom muttered his thanks and rejoined Cussy. Together they sat on a wall, devouring the printed words and dreaming of being dashing fighter pilots. Both were avid Biggles fans and knew all about it – you just wound a scarf round your neck, pulled on a pair of goggles and roared off to blast two or three Huns out of the sky before making a perfect three-pointer and toddling off for tea while the mechanics refuelled and rearmed your kite. A piece of cake.

On that balmy summer's afternoon they made their pact. They would apply and see how far along the recruiting pipeline they could travel, maybe even talk their way into uniform for a short spell. They solemnly shook hands on it.

That night in his bedroom Tom completed the form. Truthfully he stated that he had matriculated, but omitted to mention that as a bright pupil he had passed the exams two years earlier than normal. In the space reserved for his date of birth he wrote '6 May 1922', thus adding four years to his age. He slipped out of the house and posted the forms.

Two weeks later a reply came, accepting him for pilot training, provided he passed an interview and medical board at a church hall in Coventry. He was beside himself with excitement.

When he arrived – having told his mother he was out walking for the day – the medical presented no problem. The medical officer ragged him about his youthful appearance, but passed him fit for active service. It was afterwards, during the interview by the selection board that the question he had been dreading was finally directed at him. 'How old are you, Dobney?' asked a squadron leader.

'Eighteen, sir.'

'Really? Where's your birth certificate, lad?'

Tom plunged into his prepared story, looking the officer straight in the eye. 'You already have it, sir. I posted it off with my application form.'

The squadron leader sorted haphazardly through the papers littering his desk top. He had seen many candidates that day. 'Doesn't appear to be here,' he said at length. 'Still, I expect it'll turn up later.' The overworked officer had swallowed the lie, even seemed faintly embarrassed that he might have lost the document. He looked up and smiled. 'Welcome to the Royal Air Force.'

It was a tremendous moment for a boy aged just 14 years and three months. Now only one hurdle remained – he had to break the news to his mother. And that promised to be very tricky indeed. Talking her into letting him leave home would be no easy matter. She and Tom's father were separated, so the boy's departure would leave her on her own. Mrs Dobney, a former schoolteacher, was a quiet, gentle soul. Her son, on the other hand, was stubborn and determined to get his way. 'Frankly, I simply bullied her into accepting what I wanted,' Dobney told me. 'She didn't like it, but I'm afraid she didn't stand a chance. I just bullied and argued and sulked until in the end she threw up her hands and gave in. So far as she was concerned, I was joining as groundcrew. She would certainly have put her foot down and

47

stopped me on the spot had she known I was going to train as a pilot.'

On a blustery October morning in 1940, Mrs Dobney fondly kissed her son and gave him half a crown to buy sweets for the train journey to RAF Cardington, near Bedford. No. 1197690 Aircraftman Second Class Dobney, T., walked into the former airship base and into a new, adult world that was at once bewildering and exciting.

He found himself sharing a billet with men of all ages and from every walk of life. With them he queued to eat, receive his innoculations, draw a gas mask, tin helmet, boots and to try his first shuddering taste of beer in the NAAFI. He queued again one glorious, memorable day to receive his uniform. Back in the billet he slipped into the blue-grey tunic and trousers and surveyed himself gravely in a full-length mirror beneath a notice: 'Are you a credit to your uniform?'

He decided he was. The smart youth who stared out at him from the glass looked older, more capable than the sixth-former from Nuneaton. That set him thinking. *I wonder where Cussy is now?* Somewhere along the line his chum had had second thoughts about the escapade and had withdrawn. Their paths have never crossed since.

Each morning, after reveille, Tom joined his room mates at the shaving mirrors in the washrooms and went through the charade of shaving cheeks that were innocent of even the most downy fluff. Months later his single razor blade was still as keen as the day he had bought it from the NAAFI. He managed to preserve the secret of his age while square-bashing in Morecambe (Lancashire), waiting at table in the officers' mess and guarding the airfield at RAF Leuchars in Scotland, and absorbing the theory of flight in Devon.

It was not until 12 May 1941, six days after his fifteenth birthday, that he first came face to face with an aircraft. The place was No 2 Elementary Flying School, Staverton, Gloucestershire. Tiger Moth T 5714, a sweet and forgiving biplane, was as out of place in warlike camouflage as a country curate in armour. She stood on the glass, creaking and flexing her wings in a light breeze, looking pretty but frail.

Tom waddled out to her, encumbered by a bustle of parachute equipment bumping against his backside. His instructor, a middle-aged Regular, Pilot Officer Goddard, jerked his thumb towards the rear cockpit. 'Hop in, laddie,' he ordered. Tom did as he was told but was embarrassed to discover that the tiny compartment engulfed his slight frame. He could not see through the windscreen. Goddard burst out laughing, walked over to the crewroom and reappeared with two cushions which Tom stuffed beneath his parachute. Now he could clearly see the mechanic swinging the propeller and feel the blast of the slipstream in his face as Goddard taxied out for take-off. The Moth raced across the grass and the youngster experienced the greatest thrill of his life as the wheels lifted and parted from the aircraft's shadow.

Twelve flying hours and 16 days later – three weeks after his fifteenth birthday – Tom Dobney flew solo in the Tiger Moth. 'Don't bend it, son,' the instructor had said as he stepped out, leaving his pupil to it.

His landing was a sweet three-pointer – near perfect.

*   *   *

Like many other wartime fliers-in-the-making Dobney was sent to Canada where, in peaceful skies, he could perfect the techniques that would win him the coveted RAF wings. They were pinned on the left breast of his uniform at a passing out ceremony on the parade ground in Medicine Hat, Alberta. With them came, automatically, the three stripes of a sergeant pilot. He was then precisely 15 years, four months and nine days old. A few days later he was on his way back to beleaguered Britain, wondering how to explain away to his mother the proof sewn on his uniform that he was a combat flier.

'I am afraid I rather dragooned her into accepting that everything would be OK – just as I had done when I first joined up,' Dobney recalled.

'She was hurt, believing that I had misled her, but I managed to jolly her along. Perhaps it was because my father

had done exactly the same thing in the First World War –
joined as a dispatch rider when he was under age. I think,
too, she was secretly proud. Either way, she agreed to keep
my secret.'

Tom went to Bournemouth to await a new posting and
there the young airmen were paraded for a VIP inspection.
The inspecting officer, dressed in the uniform of a Marshal
of the Royal Air Force – stopped in front of Dobney.

'How are you, Sergeant?' he asked.

'Fine, sir,' Tom gulped.

The officer smiled and moved on. King George VI had
just met his youngest serviceman.

Next day Tom was posted to RAF Abingdon, Berkshire,
where he picked his crew – a navigator, wireless operator,
front gunner and rear gunner, all sergeants, from the motley
crowd. Several weeks later Dobney's Whitley lifted off the
runway for a leaflet raid on the French port of Brest. It
was the crew's very first mission over enemy-held territory.

By Bomber Command standards it was 'a piece of cake'.
No fighters, little flak and a long, unhurried run over the
town, dropping propaganda leaflets and 'window', strips of
tinfoil designed to jam enemy radar as they fluttered through
the sky. The raid was little different from the scores of training flights the crew had already completed. It was almost an
anti-climax.

'The blokes were all in their twenties, far older than me,'
Dobney said. 'But they seemed to trust me. I was a competent pilot and did the job without looking for trouble. Of
course, they would have had a blue fit if they had realized I
was still only of school age. Of course they thought I was a
trifle young-looking, but I was still the skipper.'

The second raid, a few days later, was against the shipyard
town of St Nazaire. This was the one where for the first time
Dobney came face to face with the real war. He had just
closed his bomb-doors after dropping his cargo of leaflets
when an orange glow blossomed in the sky half a mile to
starboard. A blazing British bomber tumbled gracelessly
from the formation – victim of German nightfighters. Two

minutes later the fighters 'bounced' Dobney and he turned desperately to seek the shelter of the clouds . . .

The next night, in the local pubs, the crew celebrated their safe return, but Tom's thoughts were far away from the laughter and clinking of glasses. They were back over St Nazaire and the silver ribbon of the River Loire. He was seeing again the blazing muzzles of the guns, and the pulsating inferno as the crippled British bomber caught fire. The pilot had been Gordon Hughes, a friend from the balmy training days in Canada. They had drunk together, shared the same jokes, swapped confidences and talked of what they would do after the war.

Now Gordon was dead.

'Until that moment life had been a huge adventure,' Dobney explained. 'To me the war had been like something from *Boys' Own* magazine, exhilarating, exciting and dead safe. I was convinced that I – and my mates – were invincible, that they couldn't get us.

'Only when Gordon got the chop did I begin to realize that the war was something to be taken seriously, something that could kill me.'

This sombre realization was fresh in his mind when he flew on his next raid – and his last – over St Malo. It was an easy operation and he had plenty of time to think. What he wanted, he decided, was a transfer to Fighter Command. Flying a single-engined fighter would relieve him of the awful responsibility for other men's lives that he had belatedly realized now rested on his shoulders.

Next morning he was in the bombing trainer when he was called to the CO's office. Excitedly he grabbed his cap and marched in – perhaps it was about his application to switch to Spitfires or Hurricanes. But as he stood to attention and saluted he knew that the game was up at last. A familiar figure in civilian clothes sat in a corner of the room.

'Hello, Dad,' Tom said.

His father gave a tight smile. 'How are you, son?'

The wing commander behind the desk wasted no time. 'Your father has told me your real age,' he said. 'You are too young to fly and I have no option but to ground you. Do you understand?'

The lad nodded dumbly. He had thought he was safe from his father who had not lived at home since his marriage had foundered. As though reading his son's thoughts, Herbert Dobney broke in quietly. 'I'm very sorry, Tom, but I had to tell them. By chance I met your mother and she told me where you were. You're only a boy – she shouldn't have let you do it.'

On 31 January 1942, Dobney was officially discharged by a letter from the RAF's Director of Personal Services. Part of it read . . . *the reasons . . . are solely that you are below the minimum age* . . . It went on to say that, if he rejoined at a future date, he would still be entitled to wear his pilot's 'wings'.

Soon after, a sad and chastened Tom was fretting at a workbench in a Coventry aero-engine factory. He hated the life and longed to be back in uniform. Now 16 years old, he once again faked his age and joined up. After a few weeks he was found out and returned to Civvy Street. Then, in quick succession, he joined the Fleet Air Arm, the Air Transport Auxiliary and – once more – the Royal Air Force. Each time his subterfuge was discovered. Each time he was thrown out.

Finally, towards the end of 1943, he was legally accepted into the RAF – only to crash during training at Snitterfield, Warwickshire, when an engine failed on take-off. His injuries kept him in hospital for many weeks. By the time he was fit to fly, the war was all over bar the celebrating.

In the immediate post-war era Dobney's undoubted flying skills were called on and he found himself piloting four-engined Avro Yorks into the besieged city of Berlin on the giant Allied airlift mounted to beat the Russian blockade.

He ended his career in 1950 as a pilot on the crack King's Flight, one of the Royal Family's personal pilots, and left to join the Metropolitan Police. Police life did not suit him and he again volunteered for the RAF, serving for a time as an air traffic controller before applying for his discharge and seeking new adventures in Africa.

Years later, Dobney the journalist, with a wife and five children and mellowed by the passing years, conceded that what he did was wrong.

'I was a reasonably good pilot – yes – but I was far too young to take responsibility for the safety and well-being of other, older men. I was little more than a kid; it is frightening to think I was in charge of a big bomber and actually flew missions over enemy territory.'

Today he no longer flies. Air corridors, international regulations, sophisticated radar networks have all, he believes, robbed the aviator of his freedom and individuality. But there is a handful of photographs and letters, a battered scrapbook and a yellowing pilot's log to remind him of his astonishing Air Force career.

Those – and that entry in the *Guinness Book of Records*.

4

Jock Menmuir –
For Those in Peril
on the Sea

Across the wintry snowscape, church bells tolled their call
to worship and in the isolated Northumbrian farmhouses the
ovens were warming in preparation for the Sunday roast.

Above, like some mammoth and graceless yellow bird,
the Sea King forged through the grey and troubled sky,
shuddering uneasily at the gusts of wind. It was a filthy
day, that Sabbath morning of 22 February 1981. Eight inches
of snow covered most of Britain and more was still falling,
driven by a 25-knot wind from the south. Every few minutes
a ferocious squall brought a complete white-out, hiding the
ground, as Flight Lieutenant John Streeter and his crew of
three flew their way through a routine training mission.

In an hour or so they would turn their 6-ton machine
towards home, RAF Boulmer, to eat their own Sunday lunch
in the crewroom of 'A' Flight, No. 202 Squadron. Meals were
always anticipated with relish, if only because they made a
welcome break in the often-tedious 24-hour spell on search
and rescue standby.

A few miles away, events were afoot that would ensure
that not one of the crew would be able to complain about
monotony that day; hectic adventure and danger lay ahead.

*   *   *

Cullercoats Bay, a rocky indentation in the coast north of Tynemouth, is a picturesque place that lies only 8 miles from the centre of Newcastle. For centuries the village has been a fishing community whose men have wrested a living from the treacherous North Sea. It is also a popular haunt of weekend anglers, Geordies and other townies who go there and hire a coble to be loaded with rods, bait, sandwiches and beer before putting to sea for a day's sport.

That Sunday morning was decidedly not fishing weather. The stiff southerly wind rated Force Six on the Beaufort Scale and came armed with sharp teeth that cut through the thickest garments. Heavily laden with snowflakes, it had sufficient power to slice off the white crests of the 12-foot waves that milled within the bay.

Into these menacing conditions a party of amateur fishermen from North Shields launched a 14-foot coble. They were James Brown, aged 45; his 18-year-old son, John; and two friends, Jim Dorman and Ron Errington. None wore a lifejacket. The seas were cold enough to kill a man within half an hour. Yet Brown and his party launched their boat, unwilling to call off the morning's fishing to which they had been looking forward.

Theirs was a fatal determination. Within minutes of battling through the rolling breakers into the open waters of the bay, a racing wave caught them, shouldering the cockleshell craft on to its side and pitching the four men over the gunwales into the incoming tide. Their cries for help were almost shredded by the moaning wind, but somehow reached ears on shore. Someone began running towards a telephone kiosk . . .

*   *   *

It was 10.05 a.m. The Sea King hung in a noisy hover over the disused airfield at Brunton, 5 miles north of Boulmer, as her crew practised winching techniques. Flight Sergeant Peter 'Jock' Menmuir, the winchman, stood in the open door, his face blotchy and red from the icy down-blast, and contemplated without enthusiasm another trip on the wire down to the white and petrified landscape 50 feet below. It was at that moment that the radio, tuned to the emergency frequency, crackled into life. *Tynemouth coastguards report a small fishing coble has overturned off Cullercoats. Four men are in the water nearby. Can you give assistance?*

Almost before Squadron Leader John Corby, the winch operator, had radioed confirmation of the signal, the Sea King, nose down, was clopping southwards at 120 miles per hour through the driving snow.

Routine training was forgotten as the crew mentally adjusted themselves to handling a real situation – none more assiduously than Jock Menmuir. He knew that within minutes he would be splashing into the chilling clutches of the sea; that whether men lived or died might depend on his skills. An experienced winchman, the 29-year-old Arbroath man had been dunked in the sea more times than he could remember; he knew that his training was the best, enabling him to cope with whatever demands might be placed upon him. But looking down at the angry waves below the speeding helicopter, he couldn't avoid a twinge of apprehension as he double-checked the equipment on which his life would soon, quite literally, hang . . .

Gasping with cold, the four men cursed and prayed as they fought to stay afloat in the tossing seas. Though the tide was coming in, it was no match for the strong and turbulent currents that slowly but inevitably pushed them away from the tantalizingly close shoreline. The waves were giving them a dreadful pounding, bursting over their heads to engulf them with suffocating force.

The youngest, 18-year-old John Brown, was fit and, of all of them, faring the best. Somehow he managed to claw his way towards one of the rock causeways that point out into the bay, like fingers on an outstretched hand. If he reached it, the causeway would be a precarious enough haven for breakers were exploding over it constantly. But a haven of a kind it would be. Crippled by cold and retching from the salt water he had swallowed, the youngster flailed his arms desperately. There was a shock of relief as one numb hand slapped against a rock. The other hand found some sort of grip and he hung there, choking, as another wave thundered over his head.

Beneath him a rising swell bunched its muscles. Floating in its embrace, blinded and winded, he felt himself being lifted. His hands scrabbled for fresh holds on the rocks, tearing his fingernails. Like a stranded crab he was pitched on to the streaming causeway, face down, totally spent, as the wave that had saved his life backed off. As he lay, retching and grey from lack of air, helping hands reached out to drag him to safety, well beyond the reach of the next wave.

In the boiling waters of the bay his father and the other two men were in grave difficulties as the cruel cold drained them of energy and forced their limbs into agonizing cramps. James Brown, hopelessly enmeshed in tangles of ropes and hampered by heavy oilskins, was unable to fight the ocean any longer. He gagged weakly as seawater rushed into his mouth, filling his lungs and stomach. It is doubtful whether he even heard the clamour of the Sea King as she hurdled the cliffs and arrowed down towards the upturned coble.

The calm voice of the copilot Flight Lieutenant Bob Neville came over the intercom as he spotted the cluster of figures on the fingers of rock. On one stood a uniformed policeman and a gaggle of fishermen, all pointing towards the whaleback hump of the coble's keel, by now barely breaking the surface of the water.

From the cabin door, Jock Menmuir, buffeted by the fierce down-draught from the 62-foot rotor, felt the reassuring slap of Squadron Leader Corby's gloved hand on the top of his white crash helmet, then he was pirouetting on the end of the wire as the winch began to unwind him towards a barely moving figure 40 feet below.

As he hit the water he gave an involuntary gasp. *God, it was bloody well freezing*! A rising wave hit him and he windmilled furiously with his arms and legs to prevent himself from spinning. Despite his 'bunny suit' (a woolly combination garment beneath his tight-fitting rubber immersion suit), the cold gnawed at him like a hungry animal. He went under, then surfaced, shaking his head to clear the stinging seawater from his eyes. He caught a blurred glimpse of an arm just a few feet away and lunged towards it.

His fingers fastened round it. *Got you*! He yanked it towards him, narrowing the gap between him and the drowning man. A white, vacant face lolled towards him. There was no movement in the body other than the involuntary responses caused by the swirl of the sea. *Christ, the poor bastard's dead already*.

He stared grimly into the upturned, unseeing eyes as he twisted the man's right arm anti-clockwise to lock the elbow. That way he could use its rigidity as a lever to shove him upwards and outwards while he looped the rescue strop over his shoulders. As the canvas loop slipped beneath the man's armpits, Menmuir signalled with one hand and felt the reassuring jerk of the winch tightening his harness. As they came clear of the water, he crooked his finger into the other's mouth to clear it of vomit or other obstructions before giving him the kiss of life.

To his astonishment – for he had been convinced the man was dead – the eyelids flickered open as they ascended towards the Sea King. Bawling at the top of his voice to make himself heard over the thunder of the rotor, the flight sergeant yelled: 'You're OK! Do you hear? You're OK! For Christ's sake hang on!'

He shook him vigorously. It was vital to keep him conscious so he could fight for his life against the effects of cold, shock and near-drowning. Menmuir shouted and shook him all the way up until John Corby swung them inboard to sprawl on the cabin floor. There, officer and NCO went to work on the casualty, 25-year-old Ron Errington, forcing him to vomit to clear the seawater from his system. Then on with the shouting match to stop him from slipping into unconsciousness as they packed him with blankets to provide him with life-giving warmth.

The first faint flush of colour was returning to Errington's pallid cheeks when John Corby tapped Menmuir on the shoulder and pointed out of the door. 'Look,' he said. 'There's another one!' Menmuir peered over the sill and spotted a dark blob in the white waters. Ten seconds later he was on his way down once more, though his chest still heaved from his earlier exertions.

The man, James Dorman, aged 31, was only an ace away from death. Even as the flight sergeant bobbed towards him, he slipped beneath the water until only the top of his head was showing. The winchman plopped into the water right beside him. Looping his arms round his chest, he jerked his head out of the choking waves. With the skill of long practice, he slid the strop around Dorman's shoulders and waved to the watching Corby. *Up! Up!*

He breasted the door sill and crawled into the cabin as the squadron leader eased the second rescued man to the floor. He was relieved to see that the first man he had lifted, Errington, was still alive. But his new 'client' was clearly on the brink of death, with no discernible pulse or breathing. The two airmen flung themselves at him, clamping an oxygen mask over his face and pummelling his chest to keep the heart beating.

'He looked like a goner,' Menmuir recalled. 'We knew that without hospital treatment he wouldn't last more than a few minutes. But we also knew there was another man in the water somewhere, though we couldn't see him. It was also a certainty that he was dead already. So we had to make the choice of trying to save the two who were still alive before coming back for the other man.'

Three or four minutes later, the Sea King put down in Castle Leazes Park, close by Newcastle Royal Infirmary, where waiting ambulance men unloaded the two fishermen. All that now remained was the heartbreaking task of returning to Cullercoats to search for the body of James Brown. That, at any rate, was how the RAF men saw the situation. But at that very moment a fresh drama was unfolding in Cullercoats Bay. It was almost as if the sea, having been robbed of three victims, was determined to extract full reparation . . .

As Menmuir had been fighting his battle with the waves, the men of Cullercoats lifeboat station had gallantly launched their 15 foot 6 inch rubber inshore rescue boat into the heavy seas to give what assistance they could. It had been a rough and hair-raising ride for the three crewmen, Stuart Brown,

59

Jim Griffith and Graham Boyd. Their small open boat was capable of 30 knots, and more than once they became airborne. They hung on to the bucking, flexing craft as its twin outboards sent it leapfrogging over the wave tops through the driving snow. All three men were drenched by spray and within minutes the awful cold was gnawing at their bodies.

Suddenly a freak wave, a huge hill of boiling water, reared up ahead of them, looking impossibly steep. The rubber boat clawed its way to the summit, hung there for a long moment with its engine howling, then somersaulted in an avalanche of foam, flinging her crew of three into the bay. Watchers on shore gasped as they saw the boat flop on to its back – right on top of her struggling crew.

The second 'Mayday' came as the Sea King, once more in a blinding white-out, climbed out of Castle Leazes Park, with John Streeter flying on instruments. *Inshore rescue boat overturned in Cullercoats Bay. Can you search for survivors?*

'Here we go again,' Menmuir muttered to himself. He was already exhausted and badly dehydrated by the sweat of his earlier exertions. The helicopter charged back towards the coast with wide-open throttles . . .

*   *   *

The man beneath the boat, 33-year-old Graham Boyd, was engaged in a desperate fight for his life, out of sight of his two mates. They were floundering in open water, calling his name. He was trapped in claustrophobic darkness, gasping for air and struggling to fight his way out from what shortly promised to become a rubber funeral shroud. At last his cries were heard by Jim Griffith. Despite his own fast-failing physical resources, he managed to raise one side of the boat and drag out his badly shaken shipmate. Somehow he kicked and fought his way on to the upturned keel, but when he tried to pull Boyd up beside him his muscles failed; all he could do was to yell encouragement to him and Stu Brown, bobbing and turning at the whim of the sea.

Their lifejackets, of course, would keep them afloat, but were no protection against the waves that constantly smothered them, nor against the crippling cold, nor yet against the injuries they would undoubtedly sustain were they to be flung violently against the rocks. Unless they were saved within minutes they would find themselves in the same physical state as the men they themselves had turned out to rescue.

Clinging to the tossing rubber boat, Griffith cocked his head at the rhythmic drumming of rotors; he managed a quick wave as the Sea King shot into sight above the cliffs, a patch of yellow amid flurries of white.

From the doorway, Jock Menmuir swung out. Behind him, buckled to a safety strap, Squadron Leader Corby leaned out, watching the flight sergeant's progress downwards. Through his throat mike he gave a constant barrage of course alterations for the benefit of the pilots. From his perch on the upturned boat, Griffith kept his arm outstretched, pointing towards Graham Boyd. To Menmuir and Corby the message was clear – he was indicating the man they must lift first.

The squadron leader saw with satisfaction that he had placed the winchman right on target. All Menmuir had to do was to reach out and grab his man, but when he did the lifeboatman was panicky. Small wonder after his terrible ordeal beneath the RNLI boat. He struggled furiously, almost fighting the winchman.

'Just relax, mate,' Menmuir gasped, spitting out seawater. 'Take it easy. Calm down. We'll have you out in a jiffy. Just leave it to me.' The soothing patter broke through the man's fears and Menmuir was able to guide him into the strop. Corby winched them free of the water. Dangling a few feet above the waves, they swung through the air as the Sea King clattered forward to the rock causeway where the policeman and fishermen were waiting.

Menmuir handed his charge over to them before being whisked off again to be dunked in the sea beside Stuart Brown, floating perilously close to the cruel rocks. He grabbed the lifeboatman tightly to stop him drifting away. From the doorway John Corby watched until he was sure

Menmuir had a firm grip. Then he spoke into his throat mike. 'Go forward slowly,' he told Streeter. 'We'll try to tow them to the rocks.'

Like a sportsman playing a salmon, Corby had to keep flicking the winch switch, giving them more line when they needed it, making the cable taut when necessary. All the while the machine crabbed slowly towards the reef.

A breaking wave tumbled down the length of rock. Menmuir swore as it flung them painfully against the unyielding granite. The two men found themselves rolling in a crazy, agonizing polka, whose tempo was dictated by the ebb and flow of the sea – a flurried, knee-banging, elbow-brushing affair that left them shaken and bloody. As the next wave gathered itself, Menmuir snapped out an order: 'Now – grab that rock, quick!'

Obediently the dazed lifeboatman reached for the limpet-covered boulder. The airman, like a bouncer chucking a rioter out of a nightclub, seized him by the backside and scruff of the neck and propelled him forwards and upwards to send him sprawling face down.

He staggered to his feet on the rocks, tottering like a drunk, and waved a feeble acknowledgement. Menmuir did not see it; he had already turned and was swimming with increasingly leaden limbs to the aid of Jim Griffith. With tremendous relief he saw that the third lifeboatman did not, after all, need his help. Wind and tide had fortuitously driven the RNLI boat on to the rocks and Griffith was able to step to safety. Unutterably weary, the flight sergeant was content to hang in his harness as Corby winched him back into the warmth of the cabin.

'I was damned glad that Jim had made it on his own, because the job had been the most exhausting I had ever known,' says Menmuir. 'Despite the cold I was absolutely drenched with sweat . . . all I wanted to do was to sit and have a breather.'

He flopped down on the floor. He was aching all over and breathing hard, his head bowed over his knees. But even that respite was short-lived. By now ambulances had arrived to take the shocked and freezing lifeboatmen to hospital and four times more he was winched down – thrice to lift the rescued men from their rocky perches to the waiting ambulances; the fourth time to drag their boat to the beach before the stormy seas carried it off.

Later Squadron Leader Corby was to recall: 'Jock was bushed – just about all-in. He'd done a wonderful job, working like a one-armed paperhanger for virtually every minute of the operation. But none of us wanted to quit without finding the body of the dead man. Even though we knew there was no hope for him, we had to think of the family. He was a father and a husband – his family had a right to give him the dignity of a funeral. So Jock went down again.'

That simple statement speaks volumes about the dedication and sense of duty that motivates men like Jock Menmuir. He could easily – and quite justifiably – have claimed to have done as much as could be expected of him, called it a day and flown home for a well-earned rest. But he didn't, and a couple of minutes later was once more fighting for breath in the freezing water beside the upturned coble. Clinging to its planks, he went right round it, hand over hand. *Nothing.* Then he jammed the heels of his hands beneath the gunwales, took a deep breath and lifted with all his might. He raised the starboard side a few inches out of the water and peered through the gap. *Nothing.*

He was lifted back to the helicopter and scanned the bay yet again. The grey of the sea, the black rocks, the drifting skeins of snow – everything was a blurred monochrome.

But then there was a patch of yellow: *That's him!*

Corby skilfully steered the winchman into the water, only feet from where the yellow-oilskinned figure was floating, face down, 3 feet below the surface. Once he was there, though, Menmuir could see nothing. The swirling waters were opaque, stirred up by the fierce down-draught from the Sea King's rotor.

'From 40 feet up, I could see the body clearly, but Jock was completely blind, working only by touch,' said John Corby. 'It was very frustrating watching him get so close yet unable to know which way to turn. So what I did was winch him about 10 feet out of the water, then, lowering the winch at full speed, literally lob him at the body as someone might cast a fly towards a trout.'

Menmuir was puzzled, wondering why they were lifting him, when the sudden heart-stopping fall plunged him back into the ocean. He had time only for a quick gulp of air before the waters closed over his head and realization dawned. Corby had worked out that he couldn't see and that he wasn't able to submerge of his own volition because of his lifejacket. So the winch operator was using the force of gravity to get him under.

His Mae West dragged him back to the surface. He filled his lungs with air. This time he would be ready for what he knew was coming. Corby raised him clear once more – and let him go. As he sank he opened his eyes and, through the murky waters, caught a glimpse of an indistinct yellow shape. He grabbed it and hung on as his lifejacket once more buoyed him back to the surface.

Between his fingers he felt the coarse fibres of a rope, twined round the dead man's waist. He clung to this as he felt the helicopter begin to tow them carefully towards the rocks. But after only a few yards it slipped from his numbed hands and the body sank slowly out of sight.

Again he was lifted from the water; again John Corby was right on target; again Menmuir grabbed the rope. He began hauling the corpse towards him, but with a perversity that brought a groan of frustration to his lips, the coils chose that moment to unwind.

Once more the body began to sink. Menmuir flung himself forward. His fingers fastened on the bulky oilskin. He clung on tenaciously and was relieved to feel the heavy body moving with him as the Sea King towed them to the rocks. A wave flung him against their hardness, adding to his collection of cuts and bruises. Still he held on to his pathetic bundle. Another wave struck, then another – battering and bruising him on the unyielding rock and threatening to tear the dead man from his grip.

Then suddenly the weight was gone as a forest of hands reached down and dragged him out of his arms, up on to

Wing Commander Walter 'Taff' Holden
with Lightning fighter No. XM 135 in which he took off by accident

(Express Newspapers)

Jim Clark on the winch –
showing a clear view of the wellies in which he went mountaineering!

TELEPHONE: HOLBORN 3434

Extn...............

Any communications on the
subject of this letter should
be addressed to:—
THE
UNDER SECRETARY
OF STATE, AIR MINISTRY.

and the following number
quoted:—

AIR MINISTRY,
Dept. Q.J.
LONDON, W.C.2.

31st January, 1942

No. 1197690,
Sergeant Dobney, T,
Royal Air Force.

I am directed to inform you that in carrying out
your discharge from the Royal Air Force, the reasons
which have led to this course of action are solely that
you are below the minimum age at which men are accepted
for service for air crew duties.

I am to state, however, that in view of your
having acquired all the necessary qualifications for
the award of the Royal Air Force Flying Badge you have
authority to wear the Badge on Royal Air Force uniform
should you at some future date re-enter the Royal Air
Force.

Air Commodore
Director of Personal Services
Royal Air Force

(Tom Dobney)

The letter terminating Tom Dobney's brief service as an RAF pilot –
at the age of 15

(TRH Pictures/RAF)

A Whitley bomber similar to the one captained by Tom Dobney at the age of 15

Groundcrew arm a Wellington bomber. Polish air gunner Joe Fusniak survived the crash of an aircraft like this and made an extraordinarily gallant journey through a snow storm to get help

(TRH Pictures/RAF)

the reef. A sharp tug on his harness told him that Corby was winching him in. When he reached the door, he stumbled in and dropped to the floor, fighting for breath like a beached fish. He was wearier than he had ever been in his life.

During the brief course of one hectic Sunday morning he had saved four men from drowning. Tragically, one of them, Jim Dorman, was later to die in hospital, never having woken from the coma brought about by his ordeal.

Back at Boulmer, he showered and changed before driving with the rest of the crew to the Fishing Boat Inn for a few pints. The first one slid down without touching the sides . . .

When the pub closed, someone gave Jock Menmuir a lift home. His wife Sheila smiled as he let himself in through the kitchen door.

'Hello,' she said. 'Have you had a good day?'

'Busy, love. Busy.' he replied.

5

Joe Fusniak – The Polish Air-Gunner's Loyalty

You are more than 2,000 feet above sea level, high in the desolation of the Yorkshire hills where the only sounds are the never-ceasing whine of the wind and the forlorn cry of the curlew. The walk that has brought you here has been tiring. Though little more than 4 miles, it has been uphill all the way with your feet slithering and tripping on the tussocks of hardy mountain grass that lie flat as the ears of an angry cat, pointing the way the wind has gone.

At the summit stands a stone cross, angular and black against a grey backdrop of weeping clouds. From somewhere comes a far-off drum roll of thunder. The cross is 7 foot high and perches on a cairn of local gritstone to which is affixed a polished marble tablet. Carved into it are these words:

> *Thanksgiving to God, the Parker family and local people, and in memory of five Polish RAF airmen who died here on 31.1.1942 – buried in Newark.*
>
> *The Survivor*

Here on this lonely summit, the high point between the Dales of Wharfe and Wensley, you wonder about the five men who died in such a Godforsaken spot – and about their strange memorial. So you begin to search for The Survivor.

And 300 miles away – in Kent – you track down Joseph Fusniak.

*   *   *

It was 31 January 1942, a lacklustre Saturday morning marked by leaden skies and occasional flurries of sleet. Sergeant Joe Fusniak, a 19-year-old Pole serving as an air-gunner with the Royal Air Force, was pedalling a battered Service-issue bicycle from the Sergeant's Mess at RAF Bramcote in Warwickshire towards the station briefing room. He had just finished his breakfast of bacon and egg – a privilege still afforded to all aircrew on days when they were due to fly, even in the darkest days of rationing.

Before a raid, friends would often ask each other: 'If you don't make it back, can I have your egg?' That was Bomber Command humour at its blackest – and to many the question was put only half in jest.

As Joe pedalled briskly through the cold morning air, he rounded a corner and snatched at his brakes as a blue-uniformed figure loomed dead ahead. He turned the handlebars to take evasive action, but was too late. Pedestrian, bike and rider tumbled with a crash into the road, inextricably intertwined. Fluent curses rained down on the young sergeant's head as he dragged himself and his machine upright. Mercifully, most of the tirade was wasted on him; so far his imperfect grasp of English had not encompassed the more colourful Anglo-Saxon phrases.

He stammered an apology, wincing as he slid a badly bruised leg over the crossbar of his now even more battered bike, and pedalled off for the briefing. It had not been an auspicious start to the day.

The briefing was just beginning as he arrived. He sneaked in through the door and sat at the back, nursing his bruises and stiffening leg as he tried to absorb what little he, as a tail-gunner, needed to know from all the information that was delivered from the dais – timings, courses, radio frequencies and weather forecasts.

When it was over he joined the five other members of his crew. Poles to a man, they had managed to escape to Britain to continue the fight against Hitler after the Wehrmacht had invaded their homeland in September 1939.

'Just a training flight – routine,' said Polczyk, the second pilot, a sergeant like Fusniak. He spoke in Polish, grinning as he added, in English, 'A piece of cake.' It was a new addition to their growing store of RAF slang.

Joe grinned back. For him the flight promised nothing but cramp and boredom, crouching in the tail turret of a Vickers Wellington bomber, twin .303 machine guns cocked and ready for action as he scoured the sky for the odd German raider who might chance his arm over the north of England.

It would be different soon when they would be posted to an operational squadron. Then there would be the nightly searchlights, flak batteries and shoals of nightfighters. But today offered nothing more perilous than a sedate cross-country training exercise, just part of the routine by which No. 18 Operational Training Unit sought to weld individual airmen into efficient fighting crews.

Gradually Joe was coming to know and like the other members of his crew, these five strangers to whom he had been attached in order that they might fly – and if necessary die – together. Circumstances had thrown them into each other's company, but common purpose and shared dangers had fused them into a family.

Except when transmitting radio messages in the air, when only English was permitted, they spoke entirely in Polish. Like any family, they shared jokes and were fiercely loyal to each other. Slowly they were learning English, but for all of them it was an uphill struggle and their inability to converse freely with others in the unit helped strengthen their ties even more.

The old RAF bus that circled the airfield perimeter track dropped the crews one by one near their waiting aircraft. There was horseplay and ribaldry at each stopping point. Often this was beyond the comprehension of the Polish crews who tended to be stiffer and more formal than their British counterparts. Joe and his five companions were set down beside G for George, Wellington No. 2484, as the rowdy crew bus moved on.

Fifteen minutes later they were airborne and heading north. The intercom was busy, mainly with routine instructions between the two pilots and Flying Officer Bieganski, the observer. With nothing to contribute, Joe kept silent and got on with his job – checking that the twin Brownings moved freely and that his hydraulic-powered turret would turn as required.

Like all rear gunners – 'tail-end Charlies' – he was remote form the rest of the crew who were relatively close together in the forward part of the aircraft. Separated from them by almost the entire length of the fuselage, there was little to do but scan the sky astern of the turret and try not to think of the cold.

G-George droned onwards, dipping and pitching gently on invisible currents of air. A few streaks of snow whipped past the perspex walls of his turret and Joe settled more snugly into the thick sheepskin lining of his leather flying jacket.

Over the intercom came a disembodied voice, as though someone had leaned over his shoulder to speak in his ear. 'We should be somewhere near Skipton now.' That was Bieganski working at his navigation chart. 'Keep your eyes open.'

Joe peered downwards through the snow squalls at the hilly, barren country that appeared to be slowly unwinding backwards half a mile beneath him. Nestling in a valley he saw a sizeable town. He clicked over his microphone switch. 'That must be it, Sir. Right below us, a town with a river and a railway station.'

The captain, Flight Lieutenant Kujawa, grunted an acknowledgement. Then, to Sergeant Polczyk, his co-pilot: 'Shut down the engine cowls.'

The reason for the order immediately became clear. The sky outside turned an opaque white as G-George plunged into a blinding blizzard. Huge snowflakes streaked past at the speed of tracer bullets. The cowls had to be closed to prevent the two 1,000 horsepower Pegasus engines from icing up.

Fusniak, like every other man in the crew, became instantly alert for a blinded warplane is dangerously vulnerable, both to unseen attackers and the more likely danger of mid-air collision with a 'friendly'. Rotating his turret, he quartered the sky, screwing up his eyes to try to pierce the swirling whiteness. 'But,' he was to recall many years later, employing the RAF slang he had learned with such painful slowness, 'I could not see a dickie-bird.'

Tragically for the crew of G-George, neither could the two pilots.

A heartbeat later, a brutal force seized Joe Fusniak and flung him backwards with shocking suddenness. A terrible, indescribable din seemed to fill the world. His flying helmet slammed against the turret roof. His backbone battered agonizingly on the steel hatch behind him. Inside the goldfish bowl of the turret he was flung about violently. A dreadful knifelike pain sliced through his left leg and a roaring battered at his ears.

Then, mercifully, there was silence – whiteness everywhere and a loud buzzing in his head that slowly faded as the shadows crowded in. He slid into oblivion. The time was 12.15 p.m.

*　　　*　　　*

Joe drifted towards consciousness, bewildered and at a loss to know where he was or what had happened. Slowly he identified his turret. He was sitting in it at a painful angle. It seemed to be in an odd position. Something had broken one of the perspex panels. Beyond, everything was white.

The engine noise had ceased. Now the only sound was a whine that rose and fell, the whine of a strong wind. He would go to see the others, he decided, fumbling behind his back for the catch on the steel hatch between him and the fuselage. He couldn't find it. He muttered testily as he groped for it. Then, maddeningly, he felt himself overbalancing backwards, clean out of the turret and into a drift of deep, wet snow.

For a second he blinked at the grey sky in astonishment. Then came jolting realization – G-George had force-landed. Groggily he began to struggle to his feet, only to give a shrill shout of pain as his left leg buckled beneath him. He was sent sprawling once more.

He cautiously slid his hands down his leg, aware for the first time of the sheer ferocity of the blizzard. Just below the knee he found a sharp projection – the end of a broken bone. Nausea washed over him in waves and for a moment he almost fainted. When the pain had receeded slightly he pushed himself into a sitting position and looked round, taking stock.

The turret, torn bodily from its mountings by the impact, stood lopsided in the snow like some curious igloo. A few yards away a jumble of rubble marked what was left of the drystone wall that had clawed the Wellington out of the sky. He stared at it numbly – if they had had another 3 or 4 feet of altitude they would have flown on, unconcerned and unknowing, right over the hill and back to Bramcote in time for tea.

Instead he was stuck, separated from his friends, on some bleak Yorkshire mountain, freezing cold and in pain from a broken leg. The sooner he could get the others to help him move to shelter the better. Then, when the snow had eased, they could carry him to the nearest habitation and alert the authorities.

He shouted to attract their attention but his voice was lost in the rising howl of the wind, a north-easter if the Met briefing had been accurate, he recalled. But the Met man had said nothing about it carrying icy scalpels that seemed to lay his cheeks open or about it rendering him sightless in a white fog.

Whimpering with pain as his broken leg trailed and bumped in his wake, he began to crawl through the blizzard in search of his friends. Now and again he shouted for them but each time his words were snatched away by the wind.

After a dozen yells he fancied he heard something, a deep sound almost lost in the snowstorm, that seemed to come from dead ahead. It sounded like the lowing of a cow. Heartened, he slithered towards it, for a cow offered warmth, milk and the certainty of habitation close at hand.

What he found was not a cow but the shattered hulk of G-George – clumps of torn wreckage scattered by an impact he now realized was far greater than that of any forced landing. Nothing short of a full-blown crash could have wrought such devastation.

He slid into the truncated, wingless fuselage. What seats he could see in the jumbled interior were empty; the Wellington was no more than a tube through which the gale howled with a mocking roar. The others must have taken shelter somewhere else. He shouted for them and dragged himself back into the open air. Yards beyond the shattered nose he found them, five dark bundles lying in a neat semi-circle where they had been cast in the instant of impact, their flying jackets already fading into the snowscape as fresh flakes began to cover them.

Joe reached Kujawa first. He felt for a pulse and tried not to look too closely at his skipper's injuries. There was no pulse. Sergeant Polczyk, the copilot, was dead too. Flying Officer Bieganski – dead. Sergeant Tokarzewski, the nose-gunner – dead. Sick with pain and anguish, Joe found the last of his comrades, Sergeant Sadowski, the wireless operator. Sadowski was still alive, but the snow beneath his crumpled form was slowly turning crimson.

Only then did Fusniak begin to comprehend how astonishing his own escape had been. He had been saved by his rearward-facing seat and the steel bulkhead behind it which had prevented him from being catapulted out during the fearsome deceleration from 200 miles per hour to standstill within the space of a few feet.

Unless he got help soon, however, that escape would turn out to be no more than a temporary reprieve. He could easily die in this terrible storm – as would Sadowski – if he could not find warmth, shelter and medical aid for them both. His leg was hurting like hell, but he tried to forget the waves of pain. Sadowski's grievous injuries must be his first concern. As gently as he could, he rolled the young Pole on to his back. A deep groan came from the torn mouth. So *that* had been his 'cow' . . .

With his lips close to the radio operator's ear he spoke, willing the man to listen and understand. 'I'm going to try to find the first-aid kit, then I'll see what I can do to patch you up. Do you hear me, Sadowski?' There was no answer; no flicker of recognition on the white, drawn face.

He crawled back to the hulk of the bomber, elbowing his way over sharp shards of metal until he was lying inside once more. His search yielded no morphine or bandages – only three cans of tomato soup and a parachute pack.

He stuffed the cans inside his jacket and dragged the parachute back through the deepening snow to where his fellow sergeant lay. There he tugged at the ripcord until the pack burst open and yards of silk ballooned in the wind. He caught the canopy, dragging it towards him before the gale snatched it away, using it as a blanket for the injured man. Then he propped a piece of wreckage behind his back to act as a rudimentary windbreak.

He placed one of the tins of soup nearby. 'Listen, Sadowski,' he urged. 'I am going to get help. I will not be long and you will stay warm beneath your parachute. Wait here until I return.'

The nose-gunner said nothing. Joe turned away to seek some form of support, a makeshift crutch to help him along the journey ahead. Back at G-George he used his bare hands to tear a strip of wood from the fuselage bracing. He thrust one end into the snow, tucked the other under his armpit and slowly pushed himself upright.

Only then did he feel the full fury of the blizzard. It hit him an icy hammer blow that made tears spring from his eyes, emptied his lungs and threatened to fling him on his back. He took a tentative step forward, but his flimsy crutch immediately snapped in two. He pitched headlong in the snow, screaming in agony as his wounded leg twisted beneath him. He was left clutching a remnant of wood little more than 2 feet in length. Using it like a kind of punt pole, he set off again.

Half-crawling, half-kneeling, half-fainting with pain, Joe Fusniak started out on a journey of astonishing gallantry to seek help for his dying countryman. It was a journey that was to test him to the limits of his physical and mental endurance, to take him within an ace of death and to win him an award for gallantry.

But how to start that journey? Joe had only the haziest clue as to his whereabouts; all he knew was that they had flown over Skipton about five minutes before disaster had struck.

Much later, when his terrible ordeal was over, he was to discover that the Wellington had hit the very summit of Buckden Pike, a 2,302-foot loaf-like hump 16 miles due north of Skipton at the highest point of Wharfedale. Though comparatively close to the industrial West Riding, it is countryside as bleak and wild as anywhere in the British Isles. Daunting even in midsummer, in a winter blizzard it can be as murderous as the Hindu Kush.

Instinctively the wiry Pole headed downhill – away from the claws of that Arctic wind – rolling and slithering through the snow, feeling himself weakening as pain, shock and grief began to take their toll.

What he did not know – could not know – was that he had chosen totally the wrong direction. The wind was in his face and the wind was from the north-east. In that direction lay only the lunar-like wastes of Walden Moor, scores of square miles of rolling fells, crags and deep ravines. He could crawl away into that wilderness, never to be seen again. A man could travel 8 or 10 miles before coming anywhere near a track or remote hamlet. But no man could travel 8 or 10 miles across open moorland in that weather – especially a man dragging himself along with a broken leg.

He slid further and further down the steepening slope of the Pike, deeper into a barren world where everything was white. Already, it seemed, an age had passed since he had left the site of the crash.

For no good reason he suddenly stopped. Why, he was not sure, but some instinct – some sixth sense – had taken over, warning him that no homestead, no lifeline of road, lay along the path he had chosen. With a certainty that was as strong as it was illogical, he knew he must turn back, return to the summit and start afresh. It was a heartbreaking decision to make. The half mile he had come – downhill though it was – had cost him dearly. The prospect of having to return, this time uphill, was almost too much to contemplate.

Sobbing with exertion, he began to claw his way back up the fellside, dragging himself forward a couple of feet at a time with his length of wood. His wrists shook uncontrollably under the strain and each time his broken leg twisted with his exertions, he became almost semi-conscious with pain. It seemed a never ending nightmare, that climb back to the summit, but at length he felt the chill blast of the wind grow stronger on the back of his neck and gauged that the slope was levelling off to a plateau. He knew he was close to the wreckage of G-George and paused for a moment to rub sweat from his eyes.

What he saw next undoubtedly saved his life.

It was a double line of paw-prints dotted through the snow, freshly made and as clear as the cats' eyes on the centre-line of a highway – the distinctive pad marks of a fox or a dog. In this remote spot it was almost certainly the trail of a fox.

Forgotten fragments of his days as a Boy Scout in the suburbs of Warsaw flashed into his brain. Through the weariness he searched for an elusive thought, a fact stored in the filing cabinet of his memory from some long-ago talk in the Scout hut. Something to do with foxes. But what?

Then he had it. He could remember his Scoutmaster telling them how, in bad weather, foxes will move down from the hills to slink right up to farms or even the suburbs of towns in their desperate search for food. It was a long shot, but it was all he had. Gathering up his improvised crutch, he flopped as quickly as he could through the snow, hauling himself along in the paw prints, fearful lest they be obliterated by the snowstorm.

Now his breath was rasping in painful whoops that made his chest ache. His heart and temples thudded with the punishment. His hands were frozen, swollen like balloons.

Yet still he kept moving, clinging desperately to that lifeline of shadowy indentations.

The moorland, that white and petrified moonscape, seemed to stretch to eternity. Uphill, downhill, sliding over banked-up drifts, crossing stone walls, with nothing to hear but his own sobbing breath and the scream of the wind, Joe forced himself on.

Four miles lay behind him when the paw-prints wheeled to the right. The man followed suit – then saw the reason for the change. A few feet further on, the ground just stopped. Beyond it was a void of swirling snow, a vertical drop down a rockface to an unseen quarry floor far below.

Skirting the chasm, the trail once more led downhill. The young sergeant tobogganed down the tracks, by now almost too weak to feel the throbbing pain in his petrified leg. Desperately he forced himself to go even faster for the marks were growing fainter. Without this visible proof that another creature was alive and nearby, he knew he would be lost, unable to go on. It was a hopeless race. Near the floor of the valley the trail ended. It was as though some unseen hand had plucked the fox into the sky.

Ten yards away – on the limits of visibility – was a wall. Joe wallowed forward to scale it, reaching with numb hands for its top. He overbalanced and slid into a heap at the foot. He tried again – the obstruction was no more than 4 feet high – but he might just as well have tried to climb the Eiger.

He flopped back and rested his shoulders against the uneven stones. Gentle needles pricked his eyes, forcing the lids together. A warm drowsiness began to steal through his body. Peace calmed his brain. If only he could rest here a few minutes, dozing and regaining his strength, he would be all right.

Even as he thought it, he recognized the treacherous lethargy for what it really was, but could do nothing. Death was near.

'I made my peace with God,' he recalled. 'When you are facing death – and now I knew I was – your whole life passes before your eyes. I had always thought of this as a cliché of fiction, but it is true.

76

'I remembered my parents, my childhood in Warsaw, going to school, joining the Polish Air Force, training first as a pilot, then as an air-gunner – everything.

'I began crying bitterly because I also remembered that up in the hills my friend was lying terribly injured, waiting for my help. And now I could not help him. My eyes were full of tears. I began praying again, praying the snow would stop, that somehow I would find the strength to move.

'I opened my eyes again and saw the most remarkable sight of my life. Up to that moment the whole world had been white and grey. White snow and grey clouds. Quite suddenly a gap appeared in the overcast sky and a brilliant ray of sunshine slanted down and lit up the hillside some distance away. It was an omen. From my Scripture classes I remembered that Jesus had said "I am the Light and the Way". Suddenly I felt a new strength to carry on. It flooded through me.

'I got over the wall and slid down the hill on the far side, shouting for help at the top of my voice, until I reached the bank of a stream. Somehow I managed to stand up . . . and saw figures running towards me.'

As he stood, swaying with exhaustion, his good leg knotted in an agonizing spasm of cramp and he sank to the ground. Two men bent over him. In uncertain English he croaked, 'There's an airship down.'

Nearly five hours had elapsed since the dazed sergeant had tumbled from his turret on the heights of Buckden Pike. During that time, it was later estimated, he had crawled between 4 and 5 miles.

William Parker and his brother-in-law, William Whipp, gently lifted the airman – at first they thought he was a German – and carried him to the White Lion Inn in the nearby hamlet of Cray. Parker, who was the licensee, set him down in front of a roaring fire and proffered a glass of brandy, but the Pole ignored it. Striving to speak the alien language with clarity, he told the Yorkshireman, 'Get help. There is another friend. Up on the hill.'

'Where?' asked Parker.

'On the top. The very top – get help, please.'

Only then did the Pole take a gulp of cognac, coughing as the raw spirit slid down his throat and deposited an ingot of warmth in his belly. Then he dragged a tin of tomato soup from inside his jacket. 'Please – cook,' he asked.

As the Parker family fussed around him, Joe, fearful they had not understood Sergeant Sadowski's plight, badgered them in broken English. 'Another man. On hill. Badly hurt. Get help.'

William Parker was already on his way, walking briskly through the drifting snow to the village of Buckden, 2 miles south, to find a telephone. When he raised the alarm, the Buckden village policeman, Jack Galloway, struggled to reach the wreck but was driven back by the sheer ferocity of the blizzard. A truckload of soldiers was sent from a nearby Army camp but they, too, were beaten by the weather. A local farm manager and five others, roped together for safety, tackled the Pike. Like the rest they had to admit defeat.

Finally, at 2 a.m. on Sunday morning, Bernard Close, a local landowner battled through on horseback to reach the shattered remains of G-George. But he was too late – the grievously injured Sadowski was long dead, a pathetic bundle beneath his parachute and a blanket of snow.

While successive rescue expeditions turned back in the face of the snowstorm, others were trying to get through from Skipton to Cray, a distance of 22 miles to get help to Fusniak. An RAF ambulance made the attempt, only to be abandoned in a drift. A Skipton ambulance followed. It, too, became bogged down.

Finally a Dr Cameron, a GP from nearby Grassington, drove into Cray on the heels of a snowplough and took the by now unconscious gunner to Skipton General Hospital.

When Joe came round a few hours later he found himself in one of the wards. The bed next to his was empty – awaiting the arrival of Sergeant Sadowski, a nurse told him. But Sadowski never came. Day after day, as Joe grew stronger, he pestered the staff for news of his comrade until one sat by his bedside to break the news to him that the radioman had perished alongside the rest of the crew.

It was a bitter blow. Many times in the intervening years, Fusniak has asked himself if there was not more that he could have done to save his friend. He knows he did all he could, and drove himself harder than most men could have done in that terrible storm. But almost half a century later he still mourns for Sergeant Sadowski and the others.

He remained in Skipton for seven weeks, during which time he forged friendships that have lasted to this day – with members of the Parker family who visited him regularly and the Smiths who invited him to stay at their home while his broken leg finished knitting.

When the plaster was removed he returned to RAF duties, completing his operational training. He made history by becoming the first Polish airman ever to receive the British Empire Medal, a tribute to his extraordinary gallantry from the King of his adopted country.

On 22 July 1942, almost six months after the fateful take-off from Bramcote, he was once more in the tail turret of a Wellington bomber, lifting off from RAF Hemswell, near Lincoln, with No. 301 Squadron for a night raid on Duisburg.

Close to the target his aircraft was coned by searchlights and badly damaged by flak. Fire began raging through the fuselage and the pilot ordered his crew to bale out. Before they could escape, a vast explosion blasted the Wellington to pieces.

Five of the crew died. The sixth was thrown clear, descending safely into humdrum captivity which came to an end when his POW camp was liberated by the US Army in April 1945.

Once again Joe Fusniak had demonstrated his extraordinary capacity to survive.

*   *   *

Every year since the war, demobbed and working in London as an engineer, he had travelled north to Skipton to visit those who helped save him, the hospital staff and friends he made during convalescence. The Poles are an intensely loyal nation and true friends remain friends for life. So it is with Joe and the folk of the Dales market town.

In 1973 his visit was special. That summer, helped by two companions, he toiled up the bleak slopes of Buckden Pike with the stone and cement for the memorial he had vowed to build on the spot where his comrades had died. 'They were young men who were killed a long way from their homeland,' he explained. 'They were my friends. Many people say I should forget. They accuse me of living in the past. But I cannot forget. They have to have a monument; I have to build it.'

For three days he camped in a tent on the summit that, three decades later, was still littered with scraps of G-George's wreckage. By day he worked to erect his sturdy stone cross. By night, when the unceasing wind whined and buffeted his tent, he lived with ghosts and memories.

When the monument was completed, he knelt before it and prayed for his comrades. Then he picked up his trowel and cemented his finishing touch to the base of the cairn. It was a small figurine.

Of a fox.

6

Mike Yarwood – Disaster on the Rig

Bob Neville enjoyed cooking. The other three members of his crew did not, grumbling each time they had to knock up a meal in the crewroom at RAF Boulmer. But he looked forward to it – even to the extent of taking the turn of others on occasions. Not for him simple dishes like steaks, sausages or ready-made NAAFI pies. The 35-year-old helicopter captain always strived for something special; it was a pleasant and relaxing way of filling in the long hours of boredom spent waiting for the emergency call that often never came for days or even weeks at a stretch.

Today it was chicken casserole, doing nicely as it bubbled in a slow oven. The tantalizing aroma of rich stock, herbs and simmering vegetables permeated the functional crewroom, sharpening the appetites of the RAF men who sat round, slumped in chairs, reading or dozing.

'How's it going, Egon?' enquired one.

'Coming along fine,' he announced, prodding one of the chunks of meat with an exploratory fork. 'It'll be ready pretty soon, I reckon.'

That was the precise moment the red emergency telephone chose to ring. The nearest man, Flight Sergeant Mike Yarwood, snatched up the receiver. The caller was the duty officer at the Northern Rescue Coordination Centre at Pitreavie Castle. Details were sparse. In violent weather far out in the North Sea, a ship had overturned. Survivors had been spotted in the water and a helicopter was needed to lift them to safety.

As he listened, Yarwood, a 33-year-old winchman, translated the coordinates of latitude and longitude into a chinagraph cross on his chart, pinpointing a spot some 165 nautical miles north-east of Boulmer, a remote airfield near Alnwick in Northumberland.

The others crowded round, trying to decipher his scribbled notes, knowing a call on the red phone invariably meant real work. There was Neville, the skipper, his casserole forgotten; Flight Lieutenant Mike Lakey, navigating pilot; and John Moody who operated the radio and the winch. Like Yarwood he was a flight sergeant and was also 33 years old. All served with 'A' Flight of No. 202 Squadron, Royal Air Force.

As Flight Lieutenant Neville's suppertime treat simmered slowly towards perfection, untended in the stove, they trooped outside, slamming the door of the dispersal hut behind them. Soon the windows shook to the rising whine of aero engines starting up.

*   *   *

In all the confusion Pitreavie had got it wrong. The incident to which the Boulmer chopper had been called – along with 22 other helicopters, two fixed-wing aircraft, 47 ships and three diving vessels – was not a shipwreck at all but a nightmare . . . the worst-ever oil rig disaster (until 1988's Piper Alpha tragedy), right in the heart of the big Ekofisk oilfield midway between northern Britain and Scandinavia.

Force 10 gales had been pounding the huge Meccano-like rigs. As during countless other storms the sturdy platforms, planted atop steel legs, stood firm against the howling wind and breaking waves. The accommodation modules containing offices, rest rooms and canteens were brightly lit oases of calm amid the fury of the elements.

There was one exception.

The Alexander L. Keilland – the one the oilmen had nicknamed 'Floatel' – existed as a floating hostel, providing accommodation for off-shift workers from the nearby Edda platform. Unlike the other structures that had been towed to this hostile environment in the quest for oil, she did not stand on the ocean floor. Though firmly anchored to it, she actually floated on huge, mushroom-like sponsons attached to the bottom of her five 122-foot legs that were held steady in calmer waters far below the effects of surface waves by an interlocking network of anchors and chains.

Jostled by 30-foot waves and harried by the wind, one of the tough crewboats, used for ferrying men between rigs, had smashed into one of those supporting stilts, overtaxing some of the bracing wires that helped keep it in place. The same fatal sideswipe severed one of the anchor chains, allowing the rig to swing around another of its anchor points.

The appalling weather did the rest. Like a door with one broken hinge, the whole structure began to flap, placing intolerable strains on the other 'hinges' as millions of tons of seawater crashed against the weak point. Each new racing swell made things worse, causing the structure to swing more wildly. And every swing weakened the metal more, allowing it to swing even further next time – a deadly version of the principle that enables a man to tear a beer can in half by the expedient of bending it back and forth until the metal ruptures.

The end came swiftly and savagely. Slowly at first, but then faster, the huge structure began to tilt. With a scream of tearing metal heard clearly above the roaring of the storm, the broken leg tore away, crashing beneath the waves in an explosion of foam.

Suddenly robbed of equilibrium, the rig swung uncontrollably, lurching over at an impossible angle while inside, men and equipment were hurled about like dried peas in a box. Amid terrible, harrowing scenes of death, injury and panic, the steel accommodation block slid into the ocean, turned turtle and vanished before the eyes of the incredulous witnesses who had watched helplessly from the neighbouring rig and the deck of the crewboat.

All that remained were the four sponsons, breaking the surface like vast marker buoys. The remainder of the 10,105-ton platform lay upside down – a vast steel tomb more than 100 feet below the waves.

The time was 6.31 p.m. on the evening of Thursday, 27 March 1980. In that moment, 124 men were doomed. Some died with merciful speed, knowing nothing; others perished more slowly, trapped in random pockets of air or choking in the freezing waters into which they had been flung.

Somehow a few survived. It was for these men that Bob Neville and the crew of 'Rescue 31' had been summoned – to battle the sea for their lives.

*   *   *

With flying boots clumping on the tarmac, Mike Lakey walked towards the yellow Sea King at a brisk clip, calling for the ground crew 'erks' as he went. The chopper's tanks were already three-quarters full with 4,000 pounds of aviation kerosene, but for a mission like this, so far from land, he needed every thimbleful he could squeeze in. As the airmen bustled round the fuel bowser, he climbed aboard and eased himself into the left-hand seat on the flight deck.

As the second pilot, his job was to have the twin 1,660 horsepower Gnomes 'burning and turning' when the rest of the crew boarded, to navigate throughout the operation and to take the controls when required to do so by Bob Neville. The tanker crew withdrew the hose and stood clear, and Lakey punched the starter buttons, listening to the mounting din of the turbines and watching his instruments come alive to indicate that all was well.

As Neville and the others began strapping themselves in, he cast his eyes across the isolated airfield. The cloud base was around 1,500 feet, and a gentle northerly wind was blowing between 10 and 15 knots. Although cloudy, it was dry and warm, a pleasant spring evening at the onset of twilight. It seemed impossible that, little more than an hour's flying time from there, desperate men were fighting for their lives in a North Sea storm.

Darkness was upon them when, at 7.10 p.m. 'Rescue 31', clattered into the sky, climbed to 1,500 feet and pointed her bulbous nose to the north-east. Mike Lakey punched into the keyboard of the tactical air navigation system (TANS) the last-known latitude and longitude of the 'upturned ship'. The small but efficient computer instantly fed back the two most vital facts the pilots needed to know – what course to steer and how long it would take to reach their destination.

The RAF men were still unaware of the magnitude of the disaster. The radio link by which they were able to receive updated information was complex and tortuous. Ekofisk field spoke by radio to a transmitting station in Stavanger, Norway; Stavanger was in radio contact with Pitreavie who could speak to the helicopter by high frequency radio. Soon a Nimrod would be on station with a whole array of radios and radars. Until then it was a long and shaky line of communications, which explains why the Sea King crew did not learn of their true mission until more than 30 minutes after take-off.

When, finally, they had been made aware of the sheer scale of the disaster, there was a long and impenetrable silence in the aircraft. As professional sea-watchers they had all seen the rigs of the Ekofisk field; it seemed incredible, beyond belief, that anything so vast could possibly sink.

Soon evening had turned to black night; the weather was deteriorating by the minute. With 30 miles to run to the Alexander Keilland's grave, the wind was beginning to gust strongly. The Sea King was on automatic pilot, but Bob Neville had to keep dialling in fresh heights, taking her lower each time to avoid the build-up of clouds. Before long they were down as low as 200 feet, just below the cloud base, swaying and pitching in an ever-freshening south-easterly gale.

At 8.30 a series of electronic impulses rippled through the helicopter's guidance and control systems. In just 78 seconds, without the touch of a man's hand, the Sea King automatically sank through the blackness to a height of 50 feet and her surface speed trailed away to zero. She had arrived at the spot Mike Lakey had fed into her TANS computer long ago when she was still climbing away from Boulmer.

'Rescue 31' hovered patiently, awaiting the crew's next move, in a fantastic scene like something from the set of *Star Wars*. Thousands of lights blazed all around them – lights on ships, lights on rigs, searchlights, arc lights, spotlights and flashlights – a man-made galaxy. After the disaster the field had been closed down and the gas from deep below the sea bed was being burned off; from pipes atop the rigs long streamers of orange flame were whipped by driving winds like tattered battle pennants. Normally the gas would have been pumped back underground where its pressure would help force oil to the surface. Now it was being flared off to prevent this from happening. Oil spewing out all over the place was the last thing the rescue operation needed.

Dominating all, just astern of the helicopter, was the rearing bulk of the Edda rig, sparkling like some monstrous Christmas tree ablaze with fairy lights. As the airmen carried out their hover checks they found themselves almost mesmerized by the sheer magnitude of this monument to man's quest for energy.

Their reverie was broken by a message on VHF from the scene-of-search commander in his airborne control centre, a high-flying Nimrod crammed with electronics. 'You need to be on the other side of the Edda rig. I suggest you institute a search downwind of her.' The helicopter wheeled around Edda's skyscraper-like array of lights and immediately found all that remained of the Alexander Keilland, the four monstrous sponsons – the curious 'feet' at the end of the legs. Bursting seas were breaking right over them.

'What in God's name are those?' someone asked over the intercom.

'They must be some sort of buoys for mooring ships, I suppose,' Yarwood suggested as they circled each one, searching for signs of anyone clinging to them. But there was no one; the slick surfaces were bare.

As they circled the sponsons, Mike Lakey was busy with his calculations. The wind was south-easterly, now blowing between 45 and 50 knots. Any lifeboats – or swimmers – in the water would tend to be blown towards the north-west.

'Steer three-two-zero for two miles,' he advised Bob Neville. At the end of that distance they hovered at 70 feet, their powerful searchlights criss-crossing the lashing waves. In the beams, suddenly, myriad flashes twinkled in the darkness.

Lifejackets!

Later they were to discover that every Mae West from the rig was plastered with Scotchlite reflective tape – hence the twinkling as the helicopter's lights swept over them.

'There's hundreds of 'em,' said Yarwood in wonderment from his vantage point in the open rear door on the starboard side. It was no exaggeration. They covered a quarter of a square mile, huge shoals of them jostling each other on the rising and falling seas. Each had to be flown over and examined.

Tragically each was empty. The Alexander Keilland had carried hundreds of spares and when she toppled over, the storage compartments had burst open, releasing them – every one a red herring for the rescuers. The disappointment was crushing.

'Man in the water, two o'clock!' the voice of John Moody rang in their headphones. But that, too, was a false alarm. It was an immersion suit, floating on its back, crucified to a wave and empty.

Then: 'Life-raft, three o'clock, 100 yards!' Again it was John Moody. There she was, bathed in the beam of the helicopter's noselights – a nine-man circular dinghy. Her tent-like canopy was fastened tight to keep out seawater.

Empty? Or packed with cold, frightened survivors, soaked and retching as it tossed and spun on the mounting seas? Either way they had to find out, and quickly. If there *were* men aboard they were in desperate peril. In those crashing 35-foot waves and howling winds, by now strengthened to more than 60 miles an hour, the raft could easily founder.

And even if it did not, all its occupants had already received a soaking in the freezing seas and would be suffering from the debilitating effects of hypothermia; without warm and dry clothing, death was not far away.

Then a pale hand and forearm emerged from the canopy flap and waved wildly.

'We're in business!' Yarwood shouted as he clambered into his winch harness. He had decided to use a high-line, a 120-foot length of half-inch nylon rope, looped at one end to allow it to clip on to the winch hook, lead-weighted at the other. If he could get the line to the men on the raft they could haul him inboard as the winch lowered him. Moody unplugged the winchman's helmet from the intercom, grinned and lightly punched him on the shoulder, his way of wishing his friend good luck. Then he lifted the winch switch briefly, swinging Yarwood out of the door, before clicking it down to begin the descent.

Out in the tempestuous night he spun gently on the end of the toughened wire. He had, it seemed, descended only a few feet when a huge, freak wave came avalanching towards him out of the black night. He saw the runaway monster in the glare of the lights a second or so before it engulfed him. It hit with a force that left him gasping, picking him up as a charging bull flings a matador, hurling him upwards until he was almost level with the helicopter. Just as suddenly it fell away from him.

Like some mad trapeze act he whirled back through the darkness – heading straight for the bobbing dinghy. He yelped at the body-blow as he thumped into the stout rubber. There was a painful blow on his left leg from the two-way radio strapped to his thigh. His hands raked across the yielding canopy, scrabbling for a grip. But his momentum jerked him free and he swung upwards again. *Thank God it was made of rubber,* he thought as he cartwheeled through the sky. Had it been a conventional boat, it would have almost battered him to pieces.

'I swung back again and hit the dinghy a second time,' Yarwood recalls. 'Even in the short time since I had left the aircraft I was very tired and very cold. My leg was beginning to hurt, too, where the radio had given it a thump. It must have been a hell of a blow because I soon discovered the radio was unserviceable. I had to use hand signals to get John Moody to winch me up again.'

Dripping, the aching winchman slipped on a headset to explain his problems to Moody. 'It's bloody impossible trying to winch me on to the raft,' he said. 'Put me down in the 'oggin a few yards away and I'll swim for it. Then if you get the high-line to me, I'll haul the harness in and send the blokes up one by one.'

Two minutes later he was back in the water, gasping for breath as mountains of icy water broke over him. He was reluctant to cast himself off the lifeline of the winch wire, thus severing all contact with the Sea King, but experience had already shown him he couldn't swim while encumbered by the wire and its heavy lead weight. He watched the hook swing into the sky and began a clumsy backstroke towards the dinghy.

Each winchman has his own method . . . a long time earlier Yarwood had discovered the backstroke suited him best. A mediocre performer in the baths, he had not even been able to pass the basic swimming proficiency test for membership of the local sub-aqua club when he had been stationed at Gan in the Indian Ocean. Now, trussed up in a thick rubber suit, battered by winds and waves, the few yards to the dinghy seemed as daunting as a cross-Channel swim. He was not wearing a lifejacket. He had made a conscious decision to remove it before leaving the helicopter because it would have encumbered him too much. Now he was relying only on the marginal amount of extra buoyancy afforded by his immersion suit – and his own flagging strength – to keep himself afloat.

The swim was the stuff of which bad dreams are made. Black mountains of water thundered over him as he flailed with his arms and legs to make some headway. The gale seemed to scream in fury at him. Icy cold clutched him in its ever-tightening grip. He had only one comfort – an encircling pool of light from the helicopter's searchlight that followed his slow, tossing progress along the countless ridges and valleys of the sea. By now his leg was aching abominably, his head was pounding with the exertion and he was choking and spluttering on seawater. He could hear the ragged, tearing sound of his own breath, whooping and rattling as his lungs fought for oxygen. *Too many fags*, he diagnosed bleakly.

After an eternity his numbed fingers brushed against the side of the dinghy and found a handhold. Wearily he dragged himself on a circular tour, searching for the boarding ladder. There wasn't one.

His temper flared: 'Where's the fucking ladder?' he yelled in exasperation as he trod water furiously. A head popped out of the canopy, that of a Norwegian rig worker. In passable English he said, 'It has gone. It has been torn away by the sea.'

'God, wouldn't you know it? Here, give us a hand over the side before I sink.' It took three attempts, but at last the airman slithered inboard and sprawled into the couple of inches of seawater slopping about on the floor. He lay there coughing wildly. Ten pairs of eyes watched as, like an old man, he rolled over and slowly sat up, fighting for breath. On hands and knees he crawled to the canopy flap and leaned out, bathed in a pool of light from the waiting helicopters. Fingers spread, he held up both hands. *Ten men on board*.

The helicopter wheeled nose into the wind and tracked slowly towards the bobbing dinghy. Trailing on the end of the winch wire was the high-line. Yarwood reached out for it. The two pilots were totally dependant on John Moody's instructions from the vantage point of the doorway. Calmly he directed them right over the dinghy, his voice soothing and encouraging. Moody was one of the best. The pilots had long ago learned that his quiet, unflappable voice had a balming effect; not like some winch operators who screeched in their excitement, making the men at the controls twitchy.

The high-line scraped across the top of the canopy and Yarwood grabbed it, hauling in the strop attached to the winch hook. Seconds later the first survivor was ascending, to be quickly lost from view in the eyeball-searing battery of lights beneath the Sea King. When he was safely aboard the winchman hauled in the line for the second lift and motioned another survivor towards the strop. When it was the third man's turn he suddenly stopped and asked the time. The winchman's waterproof aircrew watch showed 9.30. Said the Norwegian with feeling, 'I have been here only three hours yet it seems more like three damned years.'

Then he too was whisked upwards.

'The ten men were cold and seasick,' Yarwood said later. 'But they were a tough bunch of lads. Not one of them panicked. They all took their turn; did exactly as they were told, coming forward calmly one by one to get into the strop. Their self-discipline was impressive and it certainly helped me. The winching, once a pattern had been established, went like clockwork.'

When the tenth man had gone the stocky winchman waited until the hook was swinging down, then unsheathed his aircrew knife and sliced all the way round the dinghy. His idea was to sink it so that other rescuers would not waste time checking it out for survivors. With a bluster of escaping air, the dinghy settled quickly, becoming flaccid, wilting beneath the surface with surprising speed. It threatened to drag him down as it sank. As a swimmer fights to untangle himself from weeds, he wrestled against the clinging, rubbery embrace. A racing wave burst over him, forcing salt water into his nose and mouth. His stomach began to heave.

His strength was failing fast. He didn't think he could take much more – a fine irony, he thought, that he might choke out his last in those icy waves while the 10 men whose lives he had just saved watched from above.

'I felt all kinds of an idiot. Around me everything was turning to a can of worms, but that wasn't all – I suddenly remembered that instead of coming off the hook normally by unclipping it from my harness, I'd actually dumped the harness entirely. I'd banged the quick-release box, leaving everything dangling on the end of the wire – to make swimming easier. That was fine, but getting back was going to be an absolute sod.'

'Attaching the harness to the hook is no problem, just a click does it, but actually getting back into it was going to be a whole new ball game, especially in rough seas with hands that were numb with cold.'

He tried to will unresponsive fingers to do his bidding, but he had absolutely no sense of touch. Exhaustion washed through his body and he was virtually blind from the constant curtains of spray being dashed in his face. If he didn't manage to get himself on to the hook with some rapidity, he knew he would drown. He redoubled his efforts to force the metal tongues of the straps into the slots in the rim of the quick-release mechanism on the waistbelt.

For an age he cursed and fiddled, losing first one strap then another. Then: *Got it!* There was a click, felt rather than heard. Yarwood drew a deep breath of relief. He began semaphoring urgently to tell Moody to winch him up. Two minutes later he was being dragged into the warmth of the cabin. He fought for breath as the other flight sergeant supported him, then managed to wheeze a few words:

'That's it – I'm shattered. Absolutely bloody knackered.'

Shattered or not, he soon busied himself alongside Moody, wrapping the shivering survivors in blankets. Then, breaking one of the Air Force's cardinal rules about smoking in the air, he handed round cigarettes and took one himself. To hell with Queen's Regulations; though the first lungful of smoke made his head spin like a top, the taste was wonderful, the nicotine like balm.

Next stop was Rig H where doctors and medical facilities were waiting. TANS took them there with unswerving accuracy. Once they had touched down on the steel helipad, Yarwood stood outside the doorway, helping the survivors down. Warmer and dryer, thanks to the hot-air blowers in the cabin, the tall Norwegians smiled their thanks and patted the 5 foot 8 inch winchman on the top of his crew-cut head as they came down the steps.

'Rescue 31' was quickly on her way again, having been ordered by the Nimrod to resume the search. In the confused radio traffic came calls from a Norwegian helicopter, asking to be allowed to join the search. Mike Lakey on the radio and the crew of another RAF Sea King from Coltishall in Norfolk did their best to discourage the offer. The last thing they wanted was a strange machine, unfamiliar with RAF procedures, barging about in the dark. But someone gave the Norwegian pilot the authorization he sought. Within minutes near catastrophe brushed the Sea King, putting the lives of her crew in dire jeopardy.

The first hint was Moody speaking urgently into his microphone: 'Boss – I'm getting a very strange radar return at two o'clock.'

The two pilots peered through their salt-caked windshields in time to see blazing lights bucketing towards them at high speed from the right. At no more than 100 feet away the Norwegian roared blindly past to be swallowed up in the night. The RAF men were badly shaked by the near-miss. 'Bugger this for a game of soldiers,' said an aggrieved Bob Neville. 'Let's get upstairs in case the twit comes back.'

They climbed hard to 2,000 feet, bursting out of cloud and fog into a brilliant moonlit night. From there they heard a series of messages from the scene-of-search commander aboard the Nimrod. Conditions, he said, had deteriorated so much that the helicopters must give up the search. The Coltishall Sea King was ordered to divert to Boulmer, but 'Rescue 31' no longer had enough fuel to reach home. She would have to land on one of the rigs and refuel there.

But now thick fog was spreading fast; one by one the rigs reported that visibility was so bad that landing was out of the question. Only one – Auk Alpha, 32 miles east-north-east of Rig H – could offer landing and refuelling facilities. Beggars cannot be choosers. With fuel reserves down to 1,500 pounds, enough for 90 minutes flying, 'Rescue 31' had no option. Mike Lakey punched the coordinates into the computer – and they were on their way, hurrying to get there before the weather clamped entirely.

Shortly afterwards the weary Sea King crew faced an agonizing dilemma. As they clattered towards Auk Alpha a faint, forlorn *bleeeeeep* came into their headphones on 243 megahertz, the distress frequency. More survivors? Or an empty boat still pushing out cries for help through its automatic locater beacon? Despite the ominous prospect of losing their only landing point, they could not ignore the plea.

The computer flew them to the spot, let them down through cloud from 2,000 feet to a hover of 200 feet. Once more Moody's sharp eyes picked something out of the turmoil of mist and spray. 'Lifeboat on the starboard bow!' he called.

A totally enclosed glass-fibre rescue craft was ploughing doggedly through the waves, making a healthy 7 knots. 'Rescue 31' reported her findings to the Nimrod and asked: 'Are they OK or is there some reason for us to put a man down?'

'Information from the oil rigs states there are two injured men aboard,' replied the Nimrod, 'and that the boat is damaged and unseaworthy.'

Still exhausted from his previous ducking, Yarwood immediately volunteered to be winched down.

His memories of his second ordeal are hazy and fragmented. Once more he was floundering in pounding seas, being towed towards the egg-like craft on the winch wire . . . then he was on the roof, releasing the hook and trying to find a way in . . . hands without feeling lost their grip on the rails and he was back in the sea . . . shouting, trying to get a grip . . . squirming to avoid the still-turning propeller . . . yelling at the seemingly deaf people inside who kept ignoring him . . .

Finally he was dragged aboard and stumbling to his feet. There were 26 men aboard – not one of them injured. The boat was perfectly seaworthy. He talked to 'Rescue 31' over his speech SARBE: 'I reckon its going to be dangerous to try to lift them off,' he said. 'They're safe enough where they are. I suggest we direct a ship to them.'

This was agreed. Once more Yarwood jumped into the sea and waited for the winch wire to pick him up. He was wearier than he could ever remember being in his life.

At midnight 'Rescue 31' touched down on Auk Alpha.

*　　　*　　　*

94

The gallantry of the crew was to be rewarded in the next Honours List – an Air Force Cross for Bob Neville, the Air Force Medal for Mike Yarwood and awards of the Queen's Commendation for Valuable Service in the Air to Mike Lakey and John Moody.

Food, however, was much closer to their hearts as they tramped into Auk Alpha's brightly lit Mess Deck and sank wearily on to four chairs around a table. A grinning cook conjured up a quartet of enormous grilled steaks, piled high with chips, mushrooms and onion rings.

'Here you are, gents,' he said. 'Get yerselves outside that lot.'

The others fell on the food ravenously, but Yarwood managed only one mouthful of prime Aberdeen Angus before pushing the plate aside. Perhaps he would feel hungry once the adrenalin had slowed down . . .

At RAF Boulmer, the crew of the Sea King from Coltishall – 'Rescue 25' – trooped into 'A' Flight's dispersal hut as the duty ground crew refuelled their machine. A wonderful aroma of cooking hung in the air. They sniffed appreciatively, remembering they had not eaten for hours. One of them tracked the delicious smell to the stove where Bob Neville's creation was still simmering oh-so-gently in the slow oven.

'Hey – grab some plates and irons,' he called to the others, casting round for oven gloves. 'I've just found us a chicken casserole.'

7

Graham Jacobs – The Parachutist's Nightmare

Like some monstrous tourniquet, the tough canvas straps of the parachute harness twisted and tightened around the young man's chest and shoulders, driving hot lances of pain through his body as he spun helplessly through the air in a nightmare that would end, he was now certain, in his death. There was no doubt in Graham Jacobs's mind. His demise, violent and messy, was no more than minutes away. Strangely, that realization brought no fear – only melancholy and an acceptance of the inevitable. There was, however, one thing he must do before he died.

The taste of blood was in his mouth as, biting his lip in deep concentration, he inched his hand towards the knee pocket of this overalls, scrabbling for the cheap ballpoint he kept clipped there. Each movement, by changing his aerodynamic profile, set him spinning in new directions, but he continued to grope for the pen with a determination that outweighed each fresh discomfort.

He *needed* that pen. In the few remaining minutes left to him before he tumbled to earth, his thoughts were not with the prospect of Eternity. Instead, they focused entirely on his resolution that he would leave one last message. It would be a message of love, a final declaration to the girl to whom he was engaged to be married. A girl called Christine.

THE PARACHUTIST'S NIGHTMARE

*   *   *

From the very start he had been hooked on that heady mixture of fear and exultation that every parachutist knows and craves as others crave narcotics . . . the first heart-stopping plunge, the sensation of floating on air, the blessed jerk when the canopy opens safely, the silent glide through the sky and the sudden speed at which the earth rushes up to meet you. It is a sport of high exhilaration, sharpened by the knowledge that death is a companion who waits a mistake away.

During Graham Jacobs's second jump there had been a hitch when his canopy had snagged in a tree, yanking him to a standstill and leaving him dangling helplessly 60 feet above the ground. But even that had done nothing to dampen the 18-year-old Royal Navy air mechanic's enthusiasm for his new-found sport. To free him they had brought a fire tender. From below, his instructor had called out directions on how to release himself – not by means of the normal quick-release box, but by unclipping shoulder buckles known by their trade name of Capewells.

The quick-release box is a metal drum sitting on the midriff, attached to the waist-belt and into which clip the other straps that make up the harness. It is released in a split second by half-turning the face-plate with one hand and striking it a smart blow with the other. This enables the wearer to divest himself of his harness. If, however, he wishes to retain his harness, he can free himself from the parachute by using his Capewells. That nugget of knowledge, a piece of wisdom the average novice would not normally possess, had on that occasion released him from an uncomfortable and undignified predicament.

Four days later, on Tuesday, 6 July 1976, it was to save his life. That was the day the wiry little Yorkshireman left his digs close to the Royal Naval Air Station near Weymouth, Dorset, to make his third jump since joining the Royal Marine Parachute Club based at Dunkeswell airfield on the outskirts of Honiton, Devon.

97

The afternoon was a real scorcher with a fierce sun blazing in a cloudless sky. There was barely a whisper of breeze and the grass of the airfield was busy with the lazy murmur of insects.

After lunch, Graham buckled himself into the network of webbing, checking and double-checking that everything was correctly in place – main 'chute on his back, the smaller emergency one clipped to his chest harness. He tightened his straps firmly and, bent like an old man within their constriction, hobbled out to the waiting aircraft, a red and white Cessna, call sign Bravo Echo X-Ray.

At the controls was a civilian pilot, Richard Brooks, who started up the 285-horsepower engine while his five passengers – four pupils and an instructor/jumpmaster – made themselves comfortable in the confines of the cabin. The little monoplane rumbled across the sunbaked earth of the grass airfield, reached flying speed, and rose lazily into the summer sky. The hands on the dashboard clock pointed to 3.15.

At 2,600 feet Richard Brooks throttled back from 100 miles per hour to the safer jumping speed of 70 and the first pupil clipped his static line – a long umbilical to open his 'chute automatically – to a steel bracket secured behind the pilot's seat. The jumpmaster, Corporal Paul Heydon, a Royal Marine Commando, positioned himself near the open door.

On his command the first man exited from the aircraft. There was a pause, then the second pupil followed. Graham, shuffling towards the open door, watched the bright orange and white blooms of their canopies flower into life below and behind. Then it was his turn.

Experiencing a faint flutter in his stomach, he clicked his static line to the anchorpoint and eased himself out of the doorway on the starboard side of the aircraft to stand on a small metal step above the mainwheel. His hands grasped the wing-strut while the slipstream whipped his cheeks a bright scarlet. Impatiently he waited for the signal that would free him from the noisy, swaying aircraft and leave him to marvel at the all-too-short silent descent.

From inside the cabin, the burly corporal grinned and yelled 'Go!' The young sailor gulped a deep breath and launched himself backwards off the step, counting out loud as he went, to time the opening of his canopy.

Dead on cue he grunted involuntarily as his harness jerked tight around him, signifying that the canopy had deployed and inflated. He waited for the familiar sensation of the world being steadied and put into its rightful place beneath him.

But something was wrong, terribly wrong, and for a minute or so the bewildered youngster could not work out what it was. By some means the roar of the Cessna's engine, which by now should have been fading, was still battering his ears; instead of descending, swinging pendulum-like in a creaking harness, he was cartwheeling horizontally through the air.

Totally disorientated and not a little afraid, he looked around him to try to unravel the mystery. It was then he saw his canopy. Instead of ballooning gently above his head it was cruelly snared, hooked over the Cessna's tailplane and firmly snagged around the castor-like tailwheel. God knows by what permutations of bad fortune it had happened, but he was lashed to the aircraft as effectively as a prisoner might be attached to a ball and chain. And he could see no means of escape.

The aircraft, wildly out of trim with a greatly increased drag factor, was falling out of the sky. The engine was screaming at full throttle as Richard Brooks fought for control, but already a considerable amount of altitude had been lost.

Yet even if the pilot somehow managed to arrest the headlong plunge and put Bravo Echo X-Ray back on the even keel, what then? He could not stay aloft for ever; yet to land with the hapless parachutist trailing behind would almost certainly sign the youngster's death warrant.

At the same time a series of interlocking and seemingly insoluble dilemmas faced Jacobs himself. He did not have a knife with him, otherwise he could have cut through the rigging lines of the snagged canopy and dropped clear to save himself with his emergency 'chute. Without his weight

99

holding the canopy over the tailplane, the slipstream would cause it to billow free and blow away. Nor could he escape by using the quick-release mechanism. To do so would be tantamount to suicide. One harness sufficed for both parachutes; he would simply fall to his death.

He was feeling giddy and focusing his eyes was becoming increasingly difficult, but it needed only the most cursory of glances to realize that Paul Heydon was not going to be able to help him either by unhooking the canopy or by cutting through its rigging lines. Then 10 or so feet between the doorway and the tailplane might just as well have been 10 miles.

Barring a miracle, the expanse of nylon that should have been his lifeline would become his shroud.

* * *

In the pilot's seat Richard Brooks, a 38-year-old businessman from Chard, Somerset, saw the hunched figure fly off the wing-strut as Corporal Heydon shouted 'Go!' Almost immediately a terrific jolt shook the airframe and he was pitched forward in his safety harness. It was as though they had collided with some invisible wall. The Cessna seemed to stop in the sky. Her port wing dropped, the nose dipped violently and she wallowed her way into the threshold of what promised to be a vicious stall.

Baffled by the suddenness of it all, his eyes shot to the instrument panel. The engine continued to blare healthily, confirmed by the readings of the rev-counter, oil pressure and temperature gauges – all normal. Yet the altimeter was unwinding fast, the stall warning hooter was shrieking and the artificial horizon had gone haywire.

More mystified than afraid, he slammed the thottle lever wide open, but even at full power the horizon continued to slip higher up the windscreen until there was no blue sky to be seen, only the red soil of Devon rising to meet him. The control column bucked in his grip and he tramped hard on the right rudder pedal as he fought to halt the leftwards roll and coax her out of the headlong dive.

It was Heydon's voice, bellowing as though giving parade ground orders that told him what was wrong: 'Shit, we've got a bloody hangup!'

Still Bravo Echo X-Ray tumbled through the warm skies towards the ground. Inconsequentially, Brooks noted that the slipstream howling in through the open door was whipping up a duststorm of grit and muck from the cabin floor.

He called a brief, calm 'Mayday!' into his microphone as he watched the earth rush upwards towards him. Ten interminable seconds later, as the altimeter needle unwound below the 800-feet mark, he felt a slight increase in the g-force as the Cessna checked its fall and began to level out. The change was barely perceptible at first, but he lowered a cautious 10 degrees of flap to give the wings more lift and the effect became more noticeable.

Then he switched on the booster pump to feed additional power to the engine and saw the altimeter check and slowly start to notch up precious gains in height. The stall warning was still whooping in nerve-shredding fashion, but now the plane was climbing, in however ungainly a fashion, while the airspeed indicator was showing around 80 miles per hour.

She was an absolute cow to fly but at least she was flying. Brooks sweated as he continued to kick against the right rudder pedal to counteract the leftward jamming of the rudder caused by the pressure of the parachute canopy. Somehow he managed to get her up to 900 feet – still way below safe parachuting height – but that was her limit. She would climb no more. The engine, heavily under strain, was fast getting hot. Soon it would overheat and its oil would begin to lose viscosity. It would then be only a matter of time before something vital broke or seized up. Yet even at full throttle they were mushing along at little more than stalling speed.

For the time being at least there was little he could do but fly straight and level, putting the machine under as little stress as possible – and explain to those on the ground what had happened. He began to transmit on his radio . . .

*　　　*　　　*

Grey with shock and nausea, Graham Jacobs spun with the twisting and untwisting of the rigging lines like some spinning lure on a giant fishing line. His ears ached abominably as the slipstream forced its way under his helmet rim. His cheek hurt where it was being repeatedly slapped by a loose length of webbing. He felt sick.

'The loose strap was torture; it was driving me crazy,' he recalled. 'I found myself swearing at it because it was making me mad. Funny, that – I wasn't frightened at all, not after that first panic when I realized something had cocked up, just bloody angry with that bit of canvas.

'I suppose I was too busy to be scared, too concerned with turning over in my mind plan after plan to try to save my neck – but coming up with nothing each time.

'What was there to come up with? I couldn't use my emergency 'chute in the hope of dragging myself clear because I'd just drag the plane out of the sky altogether. I couldn't bang the quick-release box and drop clear because I'd fall out of the harness that both 'chutes were attached to. And I was too far from Paul Heydon for him to reach me.

'It was one hell of a mess. For the first time in my life I began to wonder what it would be like to die and what Chris would do when she heard I had been killed.'

He had met her at a dance a few months earlier, a slim, blonde good-looker with whom he had danced most of the evening before escorting her home to her parents' house on the outskirts of Weymouth. Christine Stanko was her name and they had been dating regularly since that night. Two months earlier she had agreed to marry him and they had begun saving up for the wedding.

A profound sadness filled him as he realized that he would probably never see her again. They had had so little time together – only weeks when they had both thought they would have years. If only he could have spoken to her just

102

once more; told her that she had been in his thoughts right to the end. Then he remembered the pen . . .

At last his fingertips fastened around it. With infinite caution he drew it from his pocket, jamming it safely between his teeth while his left hand unfastened his right sleeve and rolled the material up above the elbow. The new asymmetric shape he now presented to the slipstream caused him to spin more violently and switchback up and down, but a judicious rearranging of his limbs soon showed him how to regain a more stable position.

He removed the pen from his mouth – he is left-handed – and began to write on the skin of his right forearm. It was a slow and laborious process because every move, however slight, seemed to set him tumbling afresh. The writing was atrocious, spidery and jagged, and more than once the blunt metal tip of the ballpoint dug through his skin and drew blood. Wincing with pain he persevered. Letter by letter the message took shape in a row of crude, barely legible capitals until at last he had managed to say what was in his heart:

TELL CHRIS I LOVE HER.

The last scrawl of the final R was too much. His numbed fingers could grip the pen no longer. It was snatched from his hand and carried away by the gale of the slipstream. Somehow comforted by the knowledge that he had at least left something for Chris, Graham Jacobs braced himself for what lay ahead.

*   *   *

All hell had broken loose when Richard Brooks's 'Mayday' had alerted those on the ground, sparking off a drama the like of which the little control tower at Dunkeswell aerodrome had never before witnessed. Already the duty controller had called for help from search and rescue units of the Royal Air Force, Royal Navy and the Royal National Lifeboat Institution. The GPO had cleared all unnecessary telephone traffic off the local lines to ensure direct communications between the control tower and the rescue services.

In the tower an emergency conference was under way, dominated by the steady sweep of the second-hand of the wall clock. For already the Cessna was running critically short of fuel as the engine, still drinking the stuff as it was force-fed by the booster pump, roared flat out. Only by this means could the airborne trio hope to stay just above stalling speed.

One by one, desperate measures were discussed and rejected. At the end of a concentrated brainstorming session only three possible courses of action remained. Each was highly perilous and offered only a slim chance of salvation for the wretched Jacobs.

No. 1 – an RAF helicopter would fly in formation above the Cessna while a winchman was lowered to cut the snagged parachutist free – a plan that was to be used a few years later as the plot for one of the more improbable *Airport* movies.

No. 2 – Brooks would attempt to pancake on the flat-calm sea a few miles south of the airfield, holding the speed as low as possible in the slender hope that Jacobs would survive the impact. Even if he did, he would almost certainly drown. It was also highly likely that the aircraft would simply dig her nose into the sea and somersault at the first impact.

No. 3 – a Land Rover would chase across the airfield in the Cessna's shadow as she came into land. Four strong men standing in the back would attempt to catch the young mechanic and cut through the nylon shrouds.

All were hair-raising, all carried an uncomfortably high risk of killing not only the luckless parachutist but the pilot and, in the case of scheme No. 3, the catchers in the back of the Land Rover. Nonetheless each of the three plans was prepared, to be used if all else failed.

There was, however, one other way.

*   *   *

From the open doorway of the Cessna, Paul Heydon looked out at the pitiful bundle trailing behind the tailplane. For the first time since the bizarre accident there was a chance of saving the young Royal Navy man – but only if Jacobs could be made to understand what he must do. And understand very quickly for the engine was now overheating dangerously and gulping petrol at a fearsome rate.

Richard Brooks had already calculated they had fuel for no more than 15 minutes of flying. Once the tank emptied, the plane would *have* to go down, whether or not a solution had been found.

Corporal Heydon waved his arms, trying to attract Graham's attention, but the youngster did not see him. By now he was busy trying to cope with a new problem – he was beginning to lose his boots.

Buffeted by the 80 mile an hour slipstream, the laces had become unfastened and were now loosening fast, threatening to allow his ankle-high jump boots to slide off his feet. For some reason, it became terribly crucial that this should not happen. Graham bent to try to refasten them.

Once more the alteration to his body shape caused him to spin with renewed ferocity. He gasped for breath as he began to tumble in a series of stomach-churning barrel rolls. At first he stubbornly refused to abandon his lace-fastening attempts, but soon the bitter taste of bile warned him he might soon add to his misery by vomiting. He contented himself by curling his toes to hold his footwear in place, reflecting with macabre humour that before long he would be turning up his toes for ever . . .

For some time now a terrible thirst had assailed him. His tongue had stuck to the roof of his mouth. The bile had brought some moisture, but it had not helped; now everything tasted like the inside of a blast furnace.

'I began to daydream about drink, really fantasizing – not about anything alcoholic but about a tall, frosted glass topped up with bitter lemon and clinking with ice cubes,' he said.

'I couldn't get the thought out of my head; right then I wanted that drink more desperately than anything in the world . . . apart from getting safely to earth.'

He snapped out of his reverie as he turned his head and caught a glimpse of Paul Heydon waving to him, windmilling his arms furiously to attract his attention.

Graham waved back to show he had seen. Now the jump-master pointed to himself – *Watch me* – and began to play a desperate game of charades, miming what he wanted Graham to do with huge, exaggerated hand movements, squeezing together the thumb and first two fingers of each hand like someone clicking castanets in slow motion. Then both hands went to his shoulders, pointing to the straps of the parachute harness.

Graham watched the dumbshow in puzzlement and shook his head. Heydon groaned in frustration and went through the castanet routine again before pointing once more to his shoulder harness. At the third attempt Graham yelled out loud – realization had dawned.

Of course – the Capewells! They had got him out of a tricky spot once before; how could he, of all people, have forgotten that last-ditch escape mechanism? New hope fired him like a shot of rum warming a freezing man. He waved back wildly to show he had understood, nodding his head vigorously, not caring that the exertion had set his body switchbacking again.

All his thoughts up to that moment had been focused on the insoluble dilemma of how to free himself from the harness that pinioned him to the aircraft while somehow retaining the emergency parachute that was attached to it. By using the Capewells he could escape from the main 'chute yet keep his harness intact. Then, dropping away, there might just be time to open the second parachute before hitting the ground.

He reached up and flipped open the two safety plates that clicked down over the mechanism to prevent it from being accidentally operated. Beneath each lay two horizontally opposed buttons. Heavily spring-loaded, these were designed to be squeezed inwards between thumb and forefinger, thus releasing the anchorpoint between parachute lines and harness.

The principle was simplicity itself. Squeeze both sets of buttons simultaneously and in an instant the tether would be broken. Actuality was far different as a dismayed Graham Jacobs quickly discovered.

For a start, he was working in a highly unnatural position, lying supine in the air for some of the time and being flung about violently if he moved a limb. Then, thanks to the tourniquet effect of his harness almost cutting off his circulation, his muscles were becoming cramped and numb. He had very little feeling in his hands at all.

Worst of all, his weight, compounded by a heavy dragfactor, was putting the buckles under tremendous tension. The quick-release buttons that would normally respond to a firm squeeze would not budge, even though he pressed them with all his strength. Time and again he tried, swearing foully at them, but the strain under which they had been placed looked certain to prevent them from opening.

After that dawning of hope, it was a bleak moment.

Then . . .

With an audible *click* the right-hand Capewell flew open. A near-crippling jerk seemed to split the Yorkshireman in two. He yelled aloud as new barbs of pain shot through his chest and groin. Now he has cartwheeling through the air, dreadfully unbalanced and whirling around the left-hand buckle.

The suddenly tightened harness bit deeply into his flesh; within a few seconds it had so completely restricted his blood flow that he had lost all vestige of feeling in his legs. Sobbing with exertion, he squeezed at the remaining release buttons with all his might until his quivering hand and arm muscles ached and the veins knotted on his neck and forehead.

It was like trying to crack an almond with his bare fingers.

*   *   *

Nine hundred feet below the struggling youngster, scores of cars had squeezed on to the grass verges of narrow Devon lanes as news of the drama spread and the rubberneckers began to arrive. Hundreds of faces were upturned to watch the unfolding drama.

In the little control tower, airfield and parachute club staff listened to Richard Brooks's calm radio commentary on the fight to free Jacobs. The clock on the wall showed time was fast running out; unless he managed to release the second

Capewell within the next few minutes, they would have to attempt one of the other rescue plans.

For by then Graham Jacobs had suffered that terrifying switchback for 25 minutes.

*　　　*　　　*

Hallelujah!

The buckle clicked open. One moment it had seemed jammed for ever, impervious to all his efforts; in the next, an incredulous Graham felt himself plucked free by the slipstream.

The roar of the Cessna faded rapidly and for the first time in what felt like several lifetimes, blessed peace and silence enveloped the young mechanic as he cartwheeled lazily through the air.

The joy was shortlived. There was no time to savour his release . . . he had, he calculated, three seconds – no more – in which to deploy his reserve parachute before he fell to a bone-splintering death on the drought-baked airfield beneath.

With all his strength he yanked at the ripcord's D-ring, so hard, in fact, that his arm flailed back to its full reach. The handle kept going, flying out of his grip to spin to earth. He was falling at a speed fast approaching terminal velocity – 120 miles an hour – and the hedgerows and trees were blurred, racing towards him at breakneck speed. The wind rushed in his ears. He glimpsed upturned faces below.

The most beautiful sound in the world, like newly laundered sheets rustling in the breeze . . . another jerk at his harness . . . the spinning world suddenly transformed back into focus – and in its proper place beneath the soles of his boots . . . a frightening lurch as the canopy seemed to spill its air . . . the wonderful, lovely *plop* as it re-inflated and held him steady once more.

Now he was shouting like a lunatic, waving his arms and kicking in his exultation. 'It opened! The bloody thing opened!' he shouted. In answer came a volley of cheers from those watching on the ground, only a few feet below. He cleared his mind for the landing, bending his knees and placing his feet together, spilling air from his canopy to steer himself away from an ancient oak that was reaching up for him.

He managed to miss it, scything instead through the needle-sharp outer edges of a hawthorn to hit the ground with a solid thump that drove every breath of wind from his lungs. He lost his balance and pitched face down into a thick clump of nettles. He felt them stinging his arms and face, but cared nothing for the pain. For several minutes he just lay there, his face pressed into the dried earth, savouring the scents of summer and listening to the sleepy drone of a bumble bee.

'It was the most incredible experience of my life, like being born again,' he told me later. 'I was experiencing the sheer joy of life and a relief so strong I find it difficult to put into words. I could hardly believe I was alive.

'Ages later, I rolled over on to my back and looked up at the blue sky. There was a man standing over me.'

There was an anxious look on the farmer's tanned face that quickly turned into a broad smile. 'Hullo, son,' said the man. 'I think you'd better come with me. There's a lot of people waiting to talk to you.'

He was right. There seemed to be scores of them, all wanting to slap him on the back and pump his arm up and down, to hear his story, to buy him a congratulatory drink.

A drink!

. . . *a tall, frosted glass topped up with bitter lemon and clinking with ice cubes* . . .

'Thank you – I'd like a large bitter lemon.'

*   *   *

When it was all over, when the party had wound up, when statements had been taken for the board of inquiry, when he'd told his remarkable story for the umpteenth time, he went to the men's room and began to wash the spidery, bloodstained message from his arm.

He would tell Chris himself.

8

Jeff Todd – Hanging by a Thread

At 20,000 feet above the North Sea all was bright sunshine and brilliant blue skies – a different world from the dank, sleet-filled morning beneath the cloud cover. Like some piebald stingray, mottled grey and green, the camouflaged Victor whined through the cold, thin air, pursuing its own rippling shadow across the rumpled canopy of the clouds.

It had taken off from RAF Marham 60 minutes earlier, sloshing through slush and water lying on the runway before lifting off above the flat Norfolk landscape. At the controls was the captain, Flight Lieutenant Keith Handscomb, trussed into his ejector seat on the left of the cockpit. With him and his copilot in the cramped confines of the pressurized flight deck were three other crewmen, two navigators and an air electronics officer. They were busy – busier than the pilots who had little to do, other than make minor course changes ordered by the trio sitting hunched over their array of black boxes.

The Victor – once part of the V-bomber trinity along with the Vulcan and Valiant – was now enjoying a new lease of life as an airborne tanker, a flying filling station able to replenish combat aircraft with kerosene, so extending their operational endurance time. During this stage of the operation the pilots were little more than busdrivers while the navigators worked out the complex three-dimensional geometry involved in an airborne rendezvous.

As Handscomb kept the Victor straight and level he

watched two smaller shadows catching up with his own from behind . . . Buccaneer fighter-bombers from RAF Honington which he had been ordered to meet and refuel some 100 miles east of Newcastle-upon-Tyne. They were right on time.

Trailing behind and below the Victor's port wing, a long flexible pipe waved gently in the airflow. At the end was the Buccaneers' target, a cone-shaped drogue. Each fighter would line up in turn and ease into it the point of a metal probe set in the nose. Then, at a rate of more than half a ton a minute, the tanks would drink in fuel from the Victor's cavernous belly.

Like a humming bird probing for the nectar deep in the trumpet of a flower, the first Buccaneer closed in. There was a moment's hesitation as the probe clunked home and pushed at the flow valve deep in the drogue. Then she began sucking thirstily at the metal teat, taking on board almost a ton of fuel to replace that which she had burned during practice bombing runs at Cowden range, on the Holderness coast of Yorkshire. When his gauge showed he had accepted 2,000 pounds of kerosene the pilot throttled back and broke contact with the mother ship.

Jockeying delicately, the second pilot moved in for his turn. This was his first attempt at air-to-air refuelling. So the first two contacts would be dry . . . no fuel would be transferred until he got the 'feel' of the technique. The first run was a success. He held contact for 60 seconds before breaking off to allow the Victor to turn through 180 degrees for the second dry run.

When the tanker was heading back the way she had come, the Buccaneer pilot aimed again for the drogue, watching intently as the Victor grew larger until it filled his windshield. With a sudden shock the pilot realized he was closing far too quickly with the larger aeroplane. He snatched back on the throttles as the tip of his probe struck the drogue's rim. The pipe snaked wildly and swung inboard towards the tanker's fuselage.

The sequence of events that followed happened with bewildering rapidity. It took only a few seconds for what should have been a routine operation to turn into black tragedy. There was a loud crash as the drogue swung back and bounced on the Buccaneer's blister canopy. Still the fighter was fast overtaking the Victor; now the crescent-shaped wing was only 10 feet ahead. In a last-ditch bid to avoid a collision the Buccaneer pilot hauled back on his control column. With the hose still draped over its sturdy airframe, the fighter hurtled upwards above the tanker's wing.

Almost immediately it dropped back and down. Both crews felt a gentle tremor as the two machines touched – the underside of the Buccaneer's starboard wing dragging across the top surface of the Victor's port elevator. As the fighter banked away, the drogue snapped off the hose and whirled astern in the slipstream. The horrified Buccaneer pilot watched as a violent flutter began to shake the Victor's tailplane. He pressed his 'transmit' button and yelled a warning. But for most of the tanker crew it was too late.

Handscomb immediately ordered them to bale out but in that moment the world went beserk. There was a sudden body blow as the tail snapped off and the big machine flung its nose down with a force that hurled everyone against their safety straps. The violent manoeuvre and the sudden negative-g spelled certain death for the three men in the back of the cabin. Without ejector seats to blast them clear of the doomed plane, and unable to move against the force of several gravities, they stood no chance of reaching the emergency exit on the port side of the cabin.

In the last split second before unconsciousness washed over him, Keith Handscomb managed to overcome the terrible forces being exerted on his body and hooked two fingers round the ejector seat firing handle between his legs.

There was a sudden searing flame seen clearly by the Buccaneer crews. It turned into a pulsating glow as the tumbling machine plunged into grey cloud and exploded in a terrible fireball. At the very same instant the dark shape of an ejector seat boomeranged upwards, miraculously clearing the massive explosion.

Then – nothing.

113

The time was 12.42 p.m. The date: Monday, 24 March 1975.

*   *   *

Jeff Todd gazed out of the streaming window of the functional wooden hut, gloomily taking in the depressing scene. Rain, heavily spiked with sleet, squalled across the sodden airfield, cutting visibility to a few hundred yards. Leaden clouds hung low in the sky, moving sullenly before a spanking northerly wind. From afar came the low, menacing rumble of thunder.

He picked up the dog-eared girlie magazine he had been reading and lit a cigarette, waiting for a few minutes to tick away to 1 p.m. when his shift would end and he could go home. Until then Master Air Loadmaster Todd, a helicopter winchman serving with 'A' Flight, 202 Squadron, RAF Acklington, Northumberland, was on duty, rediscovering the hoary old Air Force adage that a flier's life is 90 per cent boredom interspersed with 10 per cent sheer panic.

The boredom was very short-lived.

The red emergency telephone shrilled with a suddenness that brought him involuntarily to his feet, the magazine slithering forgotten to the floor, the cigarette abandoned in an ashtray.

His navigator, Flight Lieutenant Dave McCarthy, snatched up the receiver and began scribbling furiously, copying the scrambled message from the Northern Rescue Coordination Centre at Pitreavie Castle, near Edinburgh.

'A Victor tanker callsign C1K 69 has crashed at 55 degs 10 mins north, 01 degs 10 mins east at 11.42 hours Zulu,' said the voice at the other end. ('Zulu' is Greenwich Mean Time by which all military flying is timed.)

'Two Buccaneer aircraft were refuelling in the vicinity; one is slightly damaged.'

As McCarthy noted the details, his captain, Flying Officer Dave Reid, was sprinting out to the bright yellow Whirlwind search and rescue helicopter that stood dripping on the tarmac apron outside the crewroom. As he ran he yelled for the ground crew, ordering them to top up the tanks with an extra 400 pounds of fuel.

The Gnome jet-powered Whirlwind was a sturdy, reliable craft much-loved by her crews, but she lacked endurance. The Victor had gone down close to the furthermost point of 'A' Flight's range. So Reid and his crew needed every spare ounce of fuel they could cram aboard.

Back in the crewroom Jeff Todd, at 36 the only non-officer on the three-man crew, prepared himself for the ordeal he knew lay ahead. Off came the 'scruff order' he normally wore in the crewroom – an old flying suit and battered carpet slippers. On went thermal underwear, a rubber immersion suit, rubber boots and an aircrew helmet.

McCarthy slammed down the phone and he and Todd ran out to the tarmac where Reid was already starting up the aircraft. They ducked beneath the clopping rotor blades and jumped aboard. At 1.04 p.m., four minutes after their tour of duty had officially ended, Reid and his crew were on their way, heading at their top speed of 95 knots for the coast, a couple of miles east of the airfield. Seconds later they roared across the cliffs, flying out over the white, wind-lashed waves.

Soon the Whirlwind was swaying and bouncing, lurching violently in the gusty turbulence. The cloudbase was low – around 100 feet and the stormy North Sea was constantly obscured by streaks of snow and driving spray. Reid was forced to throttle back to 80 knots. At times, he had no choice but to take his aircraft down to within a few feet of the curling wave tops, constantly changing course to pick his way round evil cumulo-nimbus clouds.

Every aviator fears these vast canyons of vapour. Churning inside the black-grey anvil shapes lie many perils – savage updraughts and turbulence that can turn an aircraft on its back or even break it up; blinding snows to block engine intakes; frightening electrical discharges and a freezing dampness that makes ice so fast you can actually watch it grow thicker, visibly changing the aerodynamic shape of your aircraft, weighing it down until it can no longer fly.

115

Transit time to the approximate position of the Victor's grave was about 76 minutes. High above them, beyond the clouds, one of several Nimrod reconnaissance aircraft was acting as an airborne operations room for the massive search that had begun within minutes of the collision. Below were two ships that had raced to the scene to offer assistance. Wallowing sickeningly, they were battering through 25-foot waves beside the only proof that the Victor had crashed there – an ominous ever-spreading oil slick leaking from its ruptured fuel tanks.

The Whirlwind began quartering the area, searching desperately for some clue to the fate of the five airmen. If there was someone down there they must find him fast. If not, he would die of exposure. And here, at the limit of its fuel range, the Whirlwind could only operate for a comparatively short time before heading for land.

'What's that out there – straight ahead?' The voice over the intercom was that of the navigator, McCarthy. From his seat on the left of the pilot he pointed with a gloved finger, never once taking his eyes off the scrap of colour he fancied he had seen tumbling in the waves.

The helicopter darted forward and hovered over the spot. What McCarthy had spotted was a multi-seat dinghy, four-fifths submerged. It had to be from the Victor.

'Jeff, I don't see anybody there,' said Reid, 'but we ought to take a look, just to be sure.' In the aftercabin Todd was already clipping his harness to the hook at the end of the winch cable. 'I'm ready when you are,' he said with a grim confidence he did not feel.

As Reid fought the elements to hold the helicopter steady at 30 feet – or rather an average of 30 feet for at times the waves piled up to within a few feet of its wheels – McCarthy scrambled out of his seat and dropped down behind it into the main cabin. There he would stand post in the doorway, watching every move below and operating the winch switch.

Todd sat with his feet dangling over the sill of the doorway. McCarthy unplugged him from the intercom system and briefly raised the winch switch. This lifted Todd's backside from the deck and swung him into mid-air. The navigator depressed the switch and, swaying and spinning in the lash of the downwash, he was inched down towards the crashing seas and the forlorn, waterlogged dinghy.

Half-blinded by driving spray, he jerked like a marionette as a rising wave smacked viciously against his legs, spinning him on the end of the line. Then everything turned grey-green. The only sound in a suddenly silent world was the seething and bubbling of seawater around the seals of his helmet. Finally he broke surface – back into a cacophony of roaring water and the ear-splitting din of the helicopter.

He was right beside the dinghy. He didn't need to look to know it was empty; what he had to do was turn it over to see if anyone was trapped underneath. He reached for it, hooking his fingers around one of the grab handles on its side and bracing himself for the exertion of lifting it.

At that moment a racing wave curled down on him, picked him up and flung him backwards with primeval fury. Unable to unlock his fingers in time the heavy dinghy went with him, dragging at his arm with muscle-wrenching force. Without warning the sea dropped away beneath him. The full weight of the dinghy came on his arm, yanking him upside down and tearing agonizingly at his back. His grip was broken and at a dizzy speed he began swinging in the opposite direction, spinning crazily through the air. Below him the sea was a blur as he went like a pendulum – cartwheeling almost as high as the helicopter.

With a jerk that jarred his teeth and sent fresh waves of pain coursing through his back muscles, the winch cable slammed into one of the helicopter's undercarriage legs. So great was the impact that seven strands of the finger-thick steel cable actually frayed and parted.

Then Todd was swinging back in the opposite arc. Abruptly, shockingly, he smashed into the steep wall of a newly formed wave. Gasping and choking, cursing the pain in his back, he clawed his way into the daylight, fighting for breath. 'Come on, you buggers,' he stuttered through clenched teeth, 'haul me up.'

As though he had heard him, McCarthy hit the switch and the battered, aching winchman was plucked free of the water

– only to witness, with horror, a new danger. Even in his groggy condition he had sensed that the cable had not been running smoothly. As he rose towards the cabin door he saw why – it was beginning to 'birdcage'. Broken steel strands were jamming against the pulley housing, curling back and knotting into a bushy tangle of steel. This would seriously weaken the cable and put a heavy strain on the winch motor.

All the way up, Todd winced as he watched the silvery strands of wire fluff out below the pulley. Would the cable hold? How many more winchings would it stand? Back aboard, he plugged into the intercom. 'That looked rough, Jeff,' said the navigator. 'Are you OK?'

'Yeah,' said the winchman flippantly. 'I was just rehearsing my new trapeze act. What about that bloody cable though? Looks hellish rough to me.'

The crewmen began discussing the state of the cable and whether, in view of the birdcaging, it would be too dangerous to attempt further winching. It was a discussion that was cut short by a radio message that brought heartening news . . . the German freighter *Hoheburg* had just found a survivor floating in his dinghy. They had managed to come alongside and were in the process of putting two men over the side to help him. But so violent were the seas that there was little chance of lifting the injured man up the pitching and rolling flanks of the ship . . . not without running the risk of causing him even more serious damage.

Todd could not risk sending down a stretcher and leaving the Germans to strap the pilot into it. Unfamiliar with the equipment, they would be likely to get the lashings wrong; despite the threat of the ever-weakening cable, the winchman knew he had to go back down. He had made no mention to the others of his back injuries, so the only question was whether the remaining strands of wire would stand up to further punishment.

A worried Dave Reid said, 'Heading for the ship now. Are you sure you're happy about going back down again, Jeff?'

'I'm not at all happy, not with that damned cable turning into spaghetti by the minute,' the winchman replied frankly.

'But it's got to be done. That poor sod won't last in these seas for long. Anyway,' he added jokingly, 'you're not allowed to consign me to the deep – you need a flag for burials at sea.'

As Reid steered the half mile to the *Hoheburg*, Todd prepared himself for another descent into the tempestuous seas. Quickly, he attached an extension strop to the winch hook – a 6-foot length of stout canvas webbing. To this he lashed a Neil-Robertson folding stretcher, inside which he tucked a two-way radio and a first aid kit. His plan was to use the extension strop as a tow-rope for the stretcher and other equipment, thereby leaving his hands free for swimming and the taxing business of getting aboard the dinghy. By the time he was ready the helicopter was hovering over the German ship.

'I was frightened by what I saw,' Todd recalled. 'The *Hoheburg* was rolling like a pig in terrible seas, heeling over so hard I could actually see the barnacles on her keel. The waves were enormous and even though the captain had turned across the wind to try to give the dinghy a lee it was taking a hell of a pounding.

'The Germans had acted quickly. They had put a larger dinghy over the side and two men had gone out in it to the injured pilot. They reckoned he was paralysed from the waist down and there was no way they were going to try dragging him up the ship's side in case they made things worse. But our bloke's dinghy was awash and they decided to transfer him into their boat where he'd at least be safer and where I'd have more room to deal with him.

'They had done what they could to make him comfortable and had tied the dinghy to the ship's rails so it couldn't drift away. With four of us pitching about in the boat it would have been too crowded, so they made room for me by climbing back aboard the *Hoheburg*.'

Descending on the end of the cable, Todd was dunked into the sea a good 25 yards from the dinghy. He quickly saw why Reid had gone no closer – the rotor tips were getting dangerously close to the madly pitching masts and yards of the topworks.

119

The pilot tried again and this time managed to put him down about 10 yards away, a comfortable distance to swim in normal circumstances. But in those bursting seas, with the weight of the extra equipment and the pain of his injured back, even that would be a demanding swim for a man who had once played water polo for the RAF. He unhooked himself from his lifeline and struck out, towing the stretcher in his wake by its extension strop, floundering and choking, half-blinded by the maelstrom. Much later, he reached the life-raft. The short swim had tested him to his limits and for several moments he clung to the raft, trying to gather strength for the final heave that would take him aboard.

Taking a deep breath, he ducked down and bobbed up, scrabbling to heave himself over the rubber wall. At last he flopped forward and sprawled in beside the injured pilot, gasping like a stranded fish. He pushed himself to his knees with difficulty, wincing at the stab of pain in his back, and examined the injured airman. Blood trickled from a cut on his brow and he had a massive black eye. His skin was cold and flaccid.

But of much more concern to Todd was the man's back injury, a not-infrequent result of the explosive acceleration of a detonating ejector seat. The body's central nervous system runs through the spine. Moving someone with a broken back can result in permanent paralysis, even death. On the other hand if he didn't move him soon, the deadly lethargy of hypothermia would kill him.

As gently as he could in that bouncing, pitching dinghy, with waves constantly crashing over him and wracked by awful seasickness, the winchman struggled with the weight of the unconscious man as he strove to slide him on to the stretcher. It seemed impossible, but then help arrived from an unexpected source. A huge wave broke, flooding the bottom of the dinghy to a depth of almost a foot – deep enough to give some buoyancy to the tanker pilot and enabling Todd to half-float him on to the stretcher.

As he fumbled with cold, numbed fingers to strap the Neil-Robertson tightly round the casualty, a gallant German seaman sprawled into the dinghy, volunteering help in passable English.

'Welcome aboard,' the RAF man croaked. 'Here, you look after him for a minute.' Turning to the remainder of the seamen on the *Hoheburg's* deck, Todd cupped his hands and yelled into the storm: 'We're no good here. Too close to the ship. When the helicopter comes back he won't be able to get near enough because of your masts. Untie us, pull us round the stern and let us drift out as far as the rope will allow. OK?' Communications were not easy but after a little pointing and pantomiming, the Germans nodded and began untying the rope. Todd turned his attentions to the injured pilot. He checked the lashings on the stretcher; they were ready to go. Then he picked up the radio: 'OK, come and get us.'

The Whirlwind, which had been orbiting the area searching for further survivors, wheeled and roared in to hover overhead. The winch hook dropped towards them and Todd and the German struggled for long minutes to clip the stretcher to it. At last it was secure. Todd hitched his own harness to the hook and, with the stretcher at the level of his midriff, punched the brave German lightly on his shoulder. *'Danke, mein Herr –'*

'Thanks for your help,' he shouted. *'Auf Wiedersehen.'*

The man grinned back and raised his thumb as the winch jerked the two RAF men into the sky. Todd held his breath as they began ascending, anxious eyes fixed on the ever-growing nightmare tangle of wire beneath the pulley housing. Every inch they rose was an inch nearer safety, but an inch nearer potential disaster. 'Let it hold just a few moments longer,' Todd prayed.

Miraculously the fast-stripping wire stood up to the double load and three minutes later they were in the Whirlwind's cabin. The door was shut and the heater was blowing at full bore. Despite his own pain and nausea, Todd set to work on the man he had snatched from the sea – cocooning him in blankets and polythene sheeting to try to keep him warm. Methodically he packed cotton wool inside the rim of his helmet and twined bandages round his neck. Then, forcing his fingers into the tight wrist seals of the man's sleeves, he bent and breathed warm air into the man's flying suit.

It was an urgent task, this fight to reverse the debilitating effect of prolonged submersion in the sea. Not only to keep the pilot alive, but to try to bring him round to learn the vital information he possessed. A few minutes later the eyes flickered open and stared blankly round the dark, reverberating cabin. 'Who are you?' Todd asked urgently. 'What's your name?' He had to put his ear close to the mouth in order to hear the weak reply. 'Keith Handscomb, Victor tanker captain.' Almost immediately he drifted back into unconsciousness.

Reid, the pilot, radioed the name and brief details of the rescue as he steered towards the nearest landfall, the Yorkshire resort of Scarborough – a landing that would give them the benefit of added speed from a stiff tailwind.

An hour later they touched down on the playing fields of the town's technical college where an ambulance was waiting to rush the flight lieutenant to hospital. Todd went with him. Weary and in pain, he needed treatment himself, but he also needed to talk with the pilot to try to discover what had happened in those last tragic seconds of the Victor's life. Perhaps Handscomb would tell him whether anybody else had managed to escape.

He paced the casualty waiting room, smoking a succession of cigarettes until a nurse come in. 'Doctor says you can see him now – just for a couple of minutes,' she said.

The winchman followed her to the injured officer's bed-side.

'Did anyone else get out, sir?' he asked gently. 'Or were you the only one?'

'I don't know,' said Handscomb wretchedly. 'I can't re-member anything about it. It's all a blank.'

'OK sir, I understand. You'd better rest now. I hope you're soon feeling better.' He turned to go.

'Just a minute, please.'

'Sir?'

'Thank you – thank you very much.'

No further survivors were found. Nor, but for a few scraps of wreckage, was the first Victor aircraft to suffer a fatal accident since they had been introduced to the tanker fleet 17 years previously.

Three months after that nightmare in the North Sea, Todd made history by becoming the first man to win a second Queen's Commendation for Valuable Service in the Air. The first had come for a spectacular rescue in October 1974 when the winchman had been lowered on to the domed roof of Leeds Town Hall to save an injured scaffolder. The second was for his gallantry in the boiling seas beside the *Hoheburg* when his life – and the injured pilot's – literally hung by a thread.

What gave him even more pleasure than the two silver oak leaves he may now wear on the left breast of his tunic was a letter from Keith Handscomb. It read:

> *I must say you were courageous beyond words to have done what you did for me. Unfortunately, I do not remember that part of the accident at all. My last re-collection was a vague image of someone in what must have been a larger dinghy or raft. I knew nothing of the helicopter journey. Next thing I remember was waking in the casualty reception at Scarborough Hospital. Please accept my eternal gratitude for all you did and went through in order to save my life.*

That was the best citation of all.

9

Tod Hilton –
The Aussie and the Walrus

From above the flat fields of the Pas de Calais came the angry howl of supercharged engines and the stutter of cannonfire as the melée of scrapping aircraft whirled in a dance of death, dodging and weaving through the canyons of clouds.

A group of French farmworkers, faces upturned to the autumn sky, watched excitedly, pointing as occasional flashes of sunlight reflected on perspex and aluminium to mark the progress of the dogfight.

One aircraft in particular was the object of their attention, an ugly, twin-engined machine with a curiously high tail-plane. For several minutes it had been twisting and ducking to escape the marauding fighters that circled and harried it mercilessly.

The watchers knew that the plane was that of a *Tommee* and had cheered each time it had seemed to be in the ascendant. But in the last couple of minutes they had looked on in silence as it became increasingly clear, even to the untutored eye, that the pack of Focke Wulfs was slowly gaining the upper hand. Scenting blood, the handful of Germans closed in for the kill like terriers, worrying and chivvying, raking the lone RAF machine with bursts of cannonshell.

Flight Lieutenant Johnny Van Schaik, serving with No. 137 Squadron at RAF Manston, Kent, employed every flying trick and unexpected manoeuvre he had ever learned in his efforts to shake off his tormentors. He was flying the odd-looking Westland Whirlwind, designed as a fighter but now used in the fighter-bomber role. During tests early in the war it had achieved two notable distinctions. First, under certain conditions, it could outstrip the formidable Spitfire, a fact which had earned it the nickname 'Crikey' (from a high-speed Shell advertisement of the day). And second, the four 20-millimetre Hispano cannon clustered in its nose cone could fire 600 pounds of shells a minute – the most devastating firepower of any fighter in the world.

But even those attributes were not enough to even up the hopeless, lopsided tournament he found himself fighting on his way home from a 'rhubarb' – a sortie over Occupied France during which the object was to bomb or strafe anything German.

He kicked the rudder and yanked the stick back into his stomach, reefing round in a tight turn as yet another Focke Wulf angled towards him, but this time he was not quick enough. A stream of cannonfire chewed hunks of metal from his plane. It shuddered violently as fist-sized holes tore through the fuselage and wings. Streams of black oil fountained from his starboard engine and the Whirlwind dropped one wing, hunched like a wounded bird.

There was another burst of fire from behind and a fresh rain of body-blows shook the airframe. Without warning, the crippled fighter-bomber flipped on her back and began to tumble gracelessly out of the scrimmage, trailing a spoor of oily black smoke in her wake.

No experienced fighter pilot will follow an injured opponent down, thereby losing the vital advantage of height and isolating himself from his comrades. The experienced Luftwaffe men knew the rules. Satisfied they had downed another 'kill', they let her go while they regrouped to go in search of fresh quarry.

They did not see the Whirlwind, far below and only a few hundred feet above the French countryside, recover and level out as Van Schaik managed to halt the sickening spin that had threatened to shake her to pieces. Nor did they see her turn shakily and begin to head west towards the French coast and home.

Even at this range the Kent beaches appeared tantalizingly close and, though his aircraft sounded like a bag of nails, the RAF man elected to try to make it. He coaxed and cajoled the sick 885-horsepower Peregrine engine but already it was beginning to clank and smoke alarmingly. Abruptly it ground to a halt. By now he was over water, limping badly as his other engine, which had sustained less damage, began to overheat.

It sounded as ropy as hell, but if only he could persuade it to keep turning for a few minutes more it would take him across this, the narrowest part of the Channel, to scrape in over the cliffs near Folkestone for a forced landing.

Cap Gris Nez was falling well behind now but the grey waters were gradually growing closer. Maimed and coughing, deteriorating fast, the warplane sank lower and lower. Belatedly Van Schaik realized that his hopes of flying back to England had been no more than wishful thinking; that he should have put down in France rather than risk a belly-landing at sea.

He tried to transmit a 'Mayday' but his radio was dead, shattered by cannonfire. That was bad news; it meant that unless any of his comrades were watching him – and he could see none – he would be on his own. No one would know where – or even if – he had ditched. Tightening his safety harness as far as it would go, he jettisoned his bullet-starred blister canopy and knocked off the fuel cocks, bracing himself for the impact as the white horses galloped towards him.

The time was 1.20 p.m. on Halloween – Saturday, 31 October 1942.

*   *   *

Tod Hilton, bored and restless with inactivity, glanced at the clock on the crewroom wall. It read 1.20. With a sigh he turned to a fresh page of *Punch,* feeling for another cigarette and the half-cold mug of tea beside him.

A tall, rangy pilot holding the rank of flying officer in the Royal Australian Air Force, 24-year-old Hilton was trussed

126

up in a flying suit, his mae west lifejacket in place around his chest. He was on air-sea rescue readiness at RAF Shoreham, a Coastal Command base near Brighton. The day had been quiet – 'bloody boring with nothing to do but catch up on paperwork,' he was to recall years later.

He was not to be bored for much longer. The well-worn *Punch* fluttered over his shoulder as the sound of the telephone bell cut through the quiet of the crewroom. In one smooth movement, the Aussie was out of the depths of his battered club armchair, snatching up the receiver and listening intently to the brief message from Ops. He slammed it back on to the cradle, grabbed his flying helmet and stuck his head round the door into the next room.

'Come on, Dizzy,' he called to the airman half-dozing in a chair in the corner. 'Get off your arse. We've got some trade.'

Flight Sergeant 'Dizzy' Seales, one-time speedway ace, now a wireless operator/air-gunner, caught up with him as he trotted across the wet grass outside the dispersal hut to the clumsy, antique-looking biplane that squatted there, its canvas wings and fuselage drumming gently in the stiffening breeze.

The Supermarine Walrus looked like a leftover from an earlier, gentler epoch of aviation, a slow and rheumaticky old lady out of place among the ever-sleeker, faster war-planes of the third year of the Second World War. Her single 'pusher' engine set behind the wings would shove her along at little better than 80 or 90 miles an hour. However, her low landing speed and good stability made her absolutely ideal for the air-sea rescue role, as did her capacity to put down on land or sea.

Almost 50 minutes and 65 miles after take-off, the lumbering seaplane touched down at Hawkinge, a coastal airfield close to Folkestone, to have her tanks topped with fuel to give her maximum endurance for what could turn out to be a long search.

As the bowser crew pumped petrol into her, Hilton and Seales made their way to air traffic control to receive the latest update on the whereabouts of the downed Whirlwind.

The news was heartening; a sharp-eyed fellow pilot from 137 Squadron, despite the demands of the battle raging around him, had managed to keep an eye on Van Schaik's machine as it fluttered down. He had watched it cross the coastline in a vain run for home and had seen the white scar as it had hit the water. He had even witnessed the pilot's escape from the flooding cockpit into his dinghy.

'She went in about three miles due west of Cap Gris Nez,' said one of the Hawkinge controllers. 'When last seen the pilot looked to be in one piece and was floating in his dinghy, not far from the aircraft. We'll give you an escort of four Spits to watch your tail while you see if you can find him and fish him out.'

Hilton drew on his cigarette. 'Do we know who it is?'

'Yes, Johnny Van Schaik, 137 Squadron. Know him?'

'Too right I do,' replied the Australian. 'He's an old mate of mine.'

Van Schaik was a tall, blond Englishman of Dutch descent. Hilton had often drunk beer with him in the past and the pair had had many a laugh in the watering holes along the south coast favoured by the RAF. That made the sortie different. This one was a personal matter.

At 3.35 the Walrus creaked down the runway and laboured her 2¼ tons of aluminium, wood and canvas into a sky that was fast turning to leaden grey as a freshening northerly wind herded clouds across the horizon. As she crossed the English coast she was joined by the four escort Spitfires, throttled right back to near-stalling in order to keep station, thoroughbred outriders for an elderly carthorse.

Hilton found Van Schaik at precisely 4 p.m. He was no more than a scrap, lost in the foam-veined coastal waters of France, who had caught the eye only because of the bright yellow blob of his rubber dinghy. Sixty feet away the tail of his Whirlwind poked out of the sea, held there by a pocket of air trapped in the rear fuselage.

Seales was beside Hilton on the flight deck, a second pair of eyes for the search. With a jubilant smile, the Australian dug the radio-man in the ribs and pointed, shouting above the roar of the engine: 'Radio base we've found him.'

(Express Newspapers)

The broken-off leg
of the Alexander Keilland oil-rig

Mike Yarwood – exhausted
after rescuing survivors from the
Alexander Keilland oil-rig disaster

(Express Newspapers)

(RAF)

A Victor tanker refuels two fighters in mid-air. When just such a mission went tragically wrong, winchman Jeff Todd made an historic rescue

Playing leapfrog through a minefield ... a Walrus amphibian of the kind that Tod Hilton flew to bring off an extraordinary air-sea rescue *(TRH Pictures)*

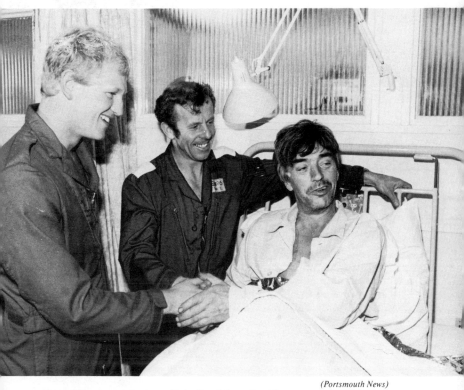

(Portsmouth News)

Steve Devereux in hospital after his ordeal in an upturned barge.
With him are his rescuers, John Spencer *(left)* and Dave Brown

(Express Newspapers)

'Amateurs . . . magnificent amateurs.' George Bain, Brian Johnstone, Alasdair Campbell and Campbell Bosanquet, with their British Airways helicopter after the *Elinor Viking* rescue

Master Air Loadmaster Dave Bullock, the winchman who gallantly gave his life trying to save a doomed US pilot

(Express Newspapers)

Seales slipped back to his own seat and began transmitting. Midway through, the radio went dead. That sudden fault was to keep it mute throughout the rest of the sortie.

Hilton sighed – gremlins at work again. He throttled back the Pegasus engine, lowered the flaps and pushed the control wheel forward. A quick touchdown beside his friend, haul him aboard and off home in time for tea. Despite the radio being unserviceable, the job was going to be a piece of cake. It would cost young Johnny a few pints in whichever Mess they ended up tonight, perhaps with the Spitfire boys who even now were climbing to give him top cover.

As the seaplane sank towards the waves, a rolling swell momentarily uncovered something that made Hilton start with sudden alarm. He clapped the throttle wide open, hauling back on the stick as the Walrus hung in the air with her engine roaring flat out. She was close to a stall.

Dead ahead, linked together like a rope of pearls, a long string of round black shapes undulated into the distance.

German mines!

He swore with some feeling and eased the nose down at a less steep angle to build up a few more knots.

At 200 feet he levelled out and began circling warily above the sodden, waving figure of his friend, searching for a spot to put down that would keep him clear of the deadly necklace. It had been an uncomfortably close escape.

From his higher elevation he saw something which had eluded him in the first shock of recognition. Two hundred yards nearer the French coast was a *second* row of the black egg-shapes. Van Schaik had managed to land bang in the middle of a full-blown minefield!

The two lines meandered, appearing roughly to follow the outline of the coast, but it was hard to be certain, for individual mines broke surface for only a moment or two each time a trough uncovered their domed tops. Certainly, the 'lane' they flanked was not straight.

Hilton's brain raced as he flew in circles above the downed pilot, examining and rejecting the options open to him. Land across the lane? Out of the question, it was far too narrow.

Go in using its length as his runway? Impossible. Whoever had heard of a meandering runway?

Head north or south to land in a safe spot above or below the field and then taxi up or down its length? That was not on either. First, he would quickly lose sight of Van Schaik and might never be able to spot him again, and second, he had no way of judging how far the minefield stretched. He might have to fly miles before finding the entrance. Third, a long taxi run, apart from squandering enormous quantities of precious fuel, would be a journey with every foot fraught with the risk of touching an unseen mine.

There was only one chance he could see: land within sight of the dinghy, but *outside* the lane – then steer through the space between two of the mines. The gap, he guessed, was less than 30 yards but wide enough providing he managed to taxi in a reasonably straight line. It would be risky, but the alternative – to fly home and report that the job was impossible – was unthinkable. Besides, Johnny Van Schaik was his mate.

The 45-foot wingspan would clear the gap comfortably under normal circumstances, but there would be nothing normal about this landing. He would be moving across the wind, across the waves, aiming for a gap he could see only in random glimpses.

'To say I was worried would be an understatement – I was scared as hell,' Hilton recalled in 1978, a few years before his death. 'In a seaplane you always tried to keep head-on to the wind and waves. Going across the weather made controlling her very difficult.

'However I decided that the only way to tackle the job was to land outside the minefield and taxi in from the west.

'I was so preoccupied and apprehensive that I made a bloody silly mistake, though it wasn't until it was all over that I realized what I'd done, that in all the uproar I had completely overlooked something vital.'

The Walrus was fitted with a sea rudder, linked to the flying controls and engaged by a lever in the cockpit. In flight this remained locked in position, but once he landed on the sea the pilot was supposed to unlock it to enable him to manoeuvre with more precision than was afforded by the mere action of propeller backwash on the aerial control surfaces. Forgetting to unlock the sea rudder meant Hilton's ability to steer through the water had been reduced to a minimum. Without its aid he would have only the most rudimentary control and would be at the whim of each wave and gust of wind.

The airman knew nothing of this as he touched down on the English side of the minefield. The landing run finished a good 20 yards short of the first row of mines. It took steady nerves to keep moving forward at 8 knots towards the hidden peril, waiting for a brief glimpse of a mine to give him an aiming point.

There!

Like a surfacing whale, a sinister black shape bobbed up 10 yards in front of the Walrus's blunt, boat-like nose. Hilton turned slightly to starboard so his port wingtip float would pass it as closely as possible. That was the one he could see best from the left-hand pilot's seat . . . hopefully the starboard one would then pass through with yards to spare.

The mine vanished again in a feather of spray. Hilton kept steering as straight a line as he could, only too conscious of the capriciousness of the elements as crosswind and current nudged and tugged at his plane. The Walrus was even more clumsy and fractious than usual, but he still did not guess at the reason.

The ugly dome bobbed up once more. With relief, Hilton watched the nearest float pass the sensitive triggering horns. There was not much room to spare – about 3 yards. At that precise instant, when muscles and nerves were wound to their tightest, a new horror manifested itself.

The lean Australian went rigid with fear. His mouth was dry and his heart raced. An appalling roar filled the cockpit, as though an express train was pounding past a few feet above his head. Instinctively he ducked. He craned his neck and saw a huge waterspout erupt from the sea a few hundred yards behind him. For a moment he thought it was an exploding mine, that somehow he had managed to touch one of them after all. Then he realized that a detonating mine would have shredded him, Seales and the seaplane.

It had been, he deduced, a shell from a German coastal battery. More, no doubt, would follow on its heels. It didn't even need a direct hit to wipe the three of them out. One shot in the right place and sympathetic detonation would do the gunners' work for them.

The Walrus was a bitch to control as she rocked and lurched across the tide, corkscrewing and dipping her wings alarmingly as she caught the brunt of the wind on her slab-like flank. Hilton realized it had pushed him too far south to reach Van Schaik. Still unaware of the forgotten sea rudder, he stood no chance of steering to the bobbing dinghy.

With a savage blast of throttle sideswiping the rudder, he turned the Walrus round and surged back the way he had come. He would try again – from open water, even though it meant braving that narrow gap once more. By half-standing, with his shoulder blades pressed against the back of his seat and feet jammed against the rudder pedals, Hilton was able to use his slightly improved view and bursts of throttle to nudge the Walrus towards the mines.

At any instant one could rear out of the water, brush the seaplane's hull and vapourize it and its occupants. As the port float slid past the horns of a mine with only a precious few feet to spare, the young Aussie cringed as another shell tore past to strike in a mushroom of foam a quarter of a mile ahead.

God, how much longer could this go on before the gunners got the range?

'Outside the channel I turned through 180 degrees and came in for another go,' said Hilton. 'She was a cow to steer – but I still hadn't twigged about the bloody sea rudder. This time, though, I was a lot happier about the run-in. Providing I didn't touch a mine, I was heading straight for Johnny. Quite quickly we came alongside his dinghy. Dizzy was in the open hatch halfway down the fuselage, waiting on the port side with a casting line.

'I throttled back. I could see Johnny waving – but he looked all in. Dizzy chucked him the hooked line and began hauling him in.'

'But the extra weight acted like a drag anchor and the nose began to swing quite violently to port – straight towards the row of mines 50 feet away. It was a nasty moment and a crushing disappointment.'

He roared down the intercom at his wireless operator: 'Let him go! We'll have to go round again'.

The NCO cast his burden adrift once more as the young officer opened the throttle and slammed hard on the right rudder. The blast from the propeller made the plane partially steerable. Once more the Adelaide-born pilot braved the gap, surging into open sea to circle round before aiming back towards the minefield.

Another shell crashed past with a fearsome din. Hilton and his wireless man flinched as it exploded behind them, noting bleakly that it had been the closest yet.

The old biplane raced forward, carving a white line across the water. It plunged past the mines on a rolling swell and surged up to the waterlogged dinghy, as neatly as an admiral's barge coming alongside. Dizzy gave a jubilant whoop as he managed to hook the fighter-pilot with a grapple. 'Got the bugger! Give us a hand, boss,' he shouted.

Hilton flung himself out of his seat and raced down the length of the flying boat to lend his muscles to the task of dragging Johnny inboard. Hand over hand, the two men hauled in the dripping rope, so fast that the huddled figure seemed fairly to plane through the water.

Van Schaik seemed far gone with cold and exhaustion as they struggled to drag him up the side but he managed a weak smile and thumbs-up sign as he slid over the raised lip around the hatch way.

'Teach you to go swimming in this weather, you old bastard,' Hilton grinned as he thumped his friend delightedly on the shoulder.

'Bollocks!' came the croaked reply.

The Australian barely heard as he dashed for the unmanned controls. He vaulted into his seat, ignoring his safety harness and fisted the throttle open, twisting his head frantically for a sight of the mines. The ungainly machine seemed to pick up speed quickly,

She was teetering along the length of a swell, both floats at times dangling clear of the water, thundering towards the explosive necklace that lurked unseen somewhere ahead.

A mine reared up. It flashed by, terrifyingly close, then they were in open water once more. Hilton remembered to draw breath again. He was drenched in sweat; the danger was beginning to wear him down.

Dizzy came forward and leaned across his right shoulder. Placing his mouth close he mouthed, 'He's OK. A few hours in bed and he'll be right as ninepence.'

Hilton nodded and pushed the throttle right through the emergency power seal. The direction was due west . . . a crosswind take-off, normally unthinkable. But Hilton didn't care any more. Anything so long as he got clear of that hellish spot as soon as possible, a million miles from those egg-shaped bastards.

Speed was building up and the biplane was riding high in the water, anxious to break free and return to her natural element.

Then it happened. Pilot and radioman gasped as a black lump of iron burst to the surface dead ahead. No more than 15 yards away. Plainly they could see the spiky horns. Another mine, – this time *outside* the minefield!

At this speed they stood no chance of stopping in time. A turn would dip a wingtip or float in the water and send them cartwheeling into a ball of wreckage. Hilton had to hold his course. Yet they were not travelling fast enough to lift over the mine, now so close it was out of sight beneath the bows.

Near-panic and sheer reflex made the Australian jerk the control column back hard into his belly. At first he did not think she would unstick but then with her nose high and tail down, the screaming seaplane staggered into the air – only to bellyflop with a shocking crash that shook every inch of her frame and threatened to amputate the floats.

But the deadly leapfrog had done the trick. They were past the mine.

More than 30 years later, Tod Hilton was unable to describe to me by what margin his aircraft had cleared the deadly hurdle. His eyes had remained tightly shut for every inch of that desperate leap.

Huge sheets of water geysered into the air as the old girl smacked into another wave, blinding the pilot as they broke over his windscreen, and echoing like a massive drumbeat on the taut canvas of the airframe. Like some ski-jump, the wave boomeranged her back into the air. She hung for a long moment before slumping back into the sea with a resounding smack.

The next bounce hurled her even higher. She faltered once more before dropping her starboard wing in the start of a stall. At this height and speed they didn't stand a cat in hell's chance; if the wingtip dug in they were all goners.

Over-correcting like mad, Tod Hilton spun the control yoke as far to the left as it would go. As his right elbow shot upwards he felt it smack into Dizzy's face. The radioman yelped and reeled back, blaspheming as he sprawled on the deck with blood cascading from his nose.

Another monumental crash shivered the Walrus as, like an urchin-flung pebble, she thumped across the waves in a wild game of ducks and drakes. For all her sedate lines, she was a tough old thing but she couldn't take much more of this cruel battering before she burst a seam, scooping up a monumental inrush of water that would literally blow her hull apart.

Yet somehow she survived each fresh skip. Five . . . six . . . seven . . .

On the eighth leap she seemed to shake herself, like a dog coming out of water. To Hilton and Seales it appeared she was sinking again. The deck dropped sickeningly beneath them and the squat nose began to plummet, this time undoubtedly to crash. They braced themselves for the impact.

It was the Walrus's very act of dropping her nose that saved them. As she began to dive, the airspeed increased by the precious few knots necessary to keep her airborne. She gathered herself and, like the grand old lady she was, turned serenely for home.

*   *   *

Months later, Tod Hilton travelled to Buckingham Palace to be decorated for bravery by King George VI who pinned upon his left breast the blue and white diagonal ribbon from which hung the Distinguished Flying Cross.

In 1946 he retired from the RAAF in the rank of wing commander. Until his death in 1984 he lived in Hertfordshire where he worked as a business consultant.

Above the fireplace in his lounge hung an ornately framed oil painting, a graphic scene of flying spray and tattered clouds. An elderly biplane is scrabbling upwards, reaching vainly for the sky above an ominous horned shape bobbing in the water.

Often, as he spoke, his gaze would turn to it, re-living the moment of terror that he never saw the first time around because Tod Hilton, the young man, had screwed his eyes tight shut.

10

Mike Lakey –
Scot of the Year

In the crowded tourist section of the British Airways Trident, Mike Lakey, an experienced RAF pilot, gritted his teeth and tightened his grip on the arms of his window seat as Flight BA 5638 from London Heathrow thumped on to the runway of Inverness Airport with a force that shook and frightened its passengers.

It was a terrible landing in atrocious weather. Out of the rain-soaked blackness, runway lights flashed by at dizzying speed as the pilot fought the savage, gusting wind to keep his rocking machine on the ground and hold it in a straight line down the centre of the concrete strip. He was braking hard as he used up the runway and there were a few murmurs of fear from the passengers, but Lakey relaxed his grip as he felt the discs biting, slowing the airliner's thumping, juddering progress to a more sedate pace.

An RAF staff car was waiting outside the arrivals lounge to take him home after a round-trip to London to attend a Press conference at which it had been announced that he and his helicopter crew were to receive an award from the Duke of Edinburgh for rescuing survivors from the ill-fated oil rig Alexander Keilland which had capsized in North Sea storms in March 1980 (see chapter 6).

Mike Lakey is a shy, reticent man and that Press conference on Wednesday, 1 October 1980, had been almost as much of an ordeal as the spectacular rescue seven months earlier. Now, as the car pulled up outside his married quarters at RAF Lossiemouth, Morayshire, he thanked his stars that he was off duty and would not have to fly again on that stormy night. He was glad to be home and was looking forward to a quiet supper with his wife, Elizabeth, while he described his day in London and told her about that bloody awful landing at Inverness.

Less than 10 minutes later the telephone rang – and Elizabeth Lakey found herself eating supper alone . . .

*　　*　　*

The alarm had been raised by the coastguard station in Orkney after the duty officer there had received a garbled emergency call from the heart of a titanic storm that was howling through the Atlantic 50 miles north-west of the island. In 70-foot waves, blasted by hurricane-force winds gusting at more than 75 miles per hour, a ship was on fire after heavy seas had smashed chemical containers and lead-acid batteries stored on her weatherdeck. The two combined to produce an explosive cocktail and within minutes the ship's centre section was burning like a blowtorch. Aboard were 22 crew, including two women and two children.

Lossiemouth had immediately launched its duty search and rescue Sea King helicopter, call sign 'Rescue 37'. With a crew of four she was already ploughing doggedly northwards into the teeth of the hurricane.

The telephone call to Lakey had been from his friend Flight Lieutenant Bill Campbell who was 'minding the shop' in 202 Squadron's crewroom at Lossiemouth. It had placed responsibility firmly on the shoulders of 32-year-old Flight Lieutenant Lakey who, in the absence of his commanding officer was the acting flight commander.

'It looks bad, Mike,' said Campbell. 'Should we rustle up a second crew in case they're needed?'

Lakey didn't hesitate. 'Yes – do that, Bill,' he replied. 'I'll call and collect Rick from his quarters; you try to find Dave. Have an aircraft standing by and I'll be there as soon as I can.'

When he arrived at Lossiemouth soon afterwards, the search and rescue hangar was booming and rattling under the hurricane's onslaught, echoing like a giant drum. Curtains of freezing rain, driven horizontally by Force 12 squalls, rattled against its steel doors. Outside on the tarmac, sodden, freezing mechanics struggled to stay on their feet as they prepared a second Sea King – 'Rescue 38' – for take-off.

Lakey, still in his best suit, had with him the man he had promised to collect, winchman Rick Bragg, a 26-year-old sergeant from Yorkshire. Waiting for them were Campbell, the winch operator, and the copilot, Flight Lieutenant Dave Simpson, whom Campbell had tracked down in the Officers' Mess. Clustered round the radio in the little operations room beside the crewroom, they listened to the details of the drama being enacted aboard the burning ship, the 15,952-ton Swedish chemical cargo carrier *Finneagle*. As the four aviators changed into flying kit they listened to radio traffic. 'Rescue 37' was making poor time because of the storm . . . a British Airways S-61 helicopter had just joined the rescue attempt . . . an RAF Nimrod reconnaissance aircraft had taken off from Kinloss to provide top cover for the operation.

At 11.10 p.m. came grave news from *Finneagle*. Another huge explosion had rocked her 590-foot length as more volatile chemicals had gone up. It was now even more imperative than before that her crew should be winched to safety. Half an hour later Lakey made a decision.

'I think we'd better pitch in with our 10 penn'orth,' he told his crew.

'Do you want to take a doctor along?' asked Campbell.

'Yes – and get Rick to sign for some morphine. There might be some injured to deal with.'

Lakey's decision to fly was made before either of the already-airborne helicopters had reached the burning ship, at a time when he had no reason to suppose they would not be able to cope. Furthermore it would rob the Lossiemouth of its stand-by search and rescue crew. If another emergency were to arise, a third scratch crew would have to be scraped together from somewhere. It was a decision which only he could make and one which, at a later date, he might be called upon to justify.

Yet had the sandy-haired pilot not gone to their aid, 22 men, women and children would almost certainly have died. For not long afterwards, when 'Rescue 37' finally reached *Finneagle,* things began to go wrong. Badly, hopelessly wrong . . .

*   *   *

At 11.55 p.m. Mike Lakey opened his throttles and 'Rescue 38' lifted from Lossiemouth's wet tarmac. He was in the captain's seat; Dave Simpson on his left. Sitting in the rear cabin with Bill Campbell and Rick Bragg was a new arrival, Squadron Leader Hamish Grant, the station medical officer, who had volunteered to fly the mission.

As they pitched and heaved through the storm they listened grim-faced to the radio reports from the rescue scene. They did not paint a very reassuring picture. The blazing ship, her crew unable to reach the engine controls, was making 8 knots, corkscrewing violently over 70-foot waves. The fire had burned through the steering linkage and her captain was having to rely on his emergency steering system to keep her head to the wind.

Time and again 'Rescue 37' had tried to lower a lifting harness to the ship, only to be beaten back by fresh billows of flames or forced to sheer off as *Finneagle's* dizzily waving radio mast threatened to knock her out of the sky. After several abortive attempts had ended in near-catastrophe, the Sea King stood off to let the civilian volunteers aboard 'Rescue 17', the British Airways S-61, have a go. They fared no better. Indeed, with their slower winch motor, shorter lifting cable and less sophisticated flying aids, they were worse placed than the RAF machine. But they stubbornly refused to quit, closing in for yet another brave attempt.

By now Lakey and his crew were close at hand, catching their first awed sight of *Finneagle* – an unearthly orange glow on the horizon, reflecting sullenly on the heaving seas and lowering storm clouds. Gradually a choking, pungent odour began to seep into the cockpit, irritating their throats and causing their eyes to water.

Dave Simpson spoke from the copilot's seat: 'Mike, I don't like the smell of that, whatever it is. It might be a good idea to bugger off out of it as fast as we can.'

Lakey didn't argue. A helicopter crewed by men ill and vomiting from chemical poisoning would be of no help to those aboard the ship. He turned left, swinging 'Rescue 38' out of the gases being driven downwind towards them, and approached the casualty in a wide, curving sweep from the south-west.

At 12.40 a.m. 'Rescue 37' had to give up the hopeless struggle. By now she was low on fuel and her crew were exhausted and shaken by their series of near collisions with *Finneagle's* radio mast. She broke off and headed for Kirkwall Airport, Orkney. 'Rescue 17' had better reserves of fuel and so remained, but was still unable to lower a line to the Swedish sailors.

'She was still there when we arrived some time after 1 a.m. – flying round in a fairly excited manner and trying to get a line down.' Lakey recalls drily. 'I've never seen anything quite like it. The ship was well alight and the glow of the flames reflected off the S-61's underside.

'*Finneagle* hit a trough, burying herself in water. But after the waves had crashed over her, she still came up blazing merrily. We were all a bit aghast at the scene. But when you see 22 people huddled on the neck of a burning ship – among them women and children – you can only put your trust in the Almighty and get on with the job.'

At a height of 200 feet he steered towards *Finneagle's* port side and hovered for five minutes while the British Airways machine made yet another fruitless attempt at rescue. From this vantage point he took stock. The Swedish ship was an incongruous-looking craft. Almost all her superstructure was in the bows, giving her a curious nose-heavy appearance. Midships was the blazing centre deck section. Aft was a low superstructure topped by a funnel, behind which was a huge stern ramp. On the bridge was a small sea of upturned, hopeful faces glowing ruddily in the light of the dancing flames.

Only one was missing – that of Captain Bertil Waenerlund, wrestling with the emergency steering in the wheelhouse. His was a crucial task; if he allowed the ship to turn her head from the oncoming mountainous seas, she would surely broach and founder under the sheer weight of water.

As he hovered Lakey glanced at his airspeed indicator. It showed 70 knots, though the helicopter was not moving – an ominous reminder of the brute of the storm into which it was flying.

The S-61 called it a day at this point, wheeling away from the ship to give 'Rescue 38' a clear field. In the rear cabin Sergeant Bragg clambered into his harness, bravely volunteering to go down to try to lift the survivors. He took a deep breath and went over the side. Almost immediately the shrieking wind flung him back towards the whirling tail rotor.

'Sod this for a lark!' he yelled. 'Winch me back in!'

His words, of course, could not be heard, but Bill Campbell, seeing the sergeant trailing almost horizontally on the end of the wire, got the message and hit the winch control.

'Rick managed a fairly close and detailed inspection of the tail rotor,' a wry Lakey recalls. 'So we got him in fast and tried to think of something else.'

The something else they decided on was a high-line. If they could somehow get this to the people below, the Swedish seamen could use it to haul in the rescue harness while Campbell paid out the wire. As Bragg lashed it in place, Lakey and Simpson made rapid calculations from their instrument readings, measuring the ship's speed, then using the sensitive radio altimeter to calculate how high she was rising when she hit a big wave. It was all rule-of-thumb stuff, but it gave the pilots some idea of the safety margins to which they would be working.

One worry, at least, had been removed. *Finneagle's* chief engineer had managed to scramble to the top of the bridge and hack down the radio mast which had been such a threat to the helicopters. Unable to reach his tool bag in the engine room, he had improvised with a meat cleaver from the galley.

Lakey nosed forward until 'Rescue 38' was flying ahead of the bows, keeping station with the runaway ship at a steady 8 knots, as Campbell began to pay out the winch wire and the whipping high-line. His was a delicate, frustrating job. Despite steadying lead weights on the end, the line was snaking wildly in the wind. He winched out slowly and a forest of arms reached out. A capricious blast of wind flicked it out of reach. Campbell groaned and tried again. Once more the outstretched hands missed by a few tantalizing inches. He steadied himself in the doorway of the swaying cabin and let out a few more feet of cable, watching the white nylon line writhe towards the figures silhouetted by the flames.

'They've got it!' he called over the intercom, feeding out more cable as willing hands pulled at the high-line to drag the rescue harness towards the bridge. At the same time Lakey gingerly changed course, moving from his position ahead of the ship to a new station off the port bow – in line with the bridge. He was only too aware that any sudden movement could snatch the slender line from the clutching hands. He crabbed sideways, constantly working the controls to try to iron out the battering body blows of the storm.

A hundred years later he was in position. 'Two people in the strops.' That was Campbell. 'Come right slowly.'

This was the tricky part. If they winched at this angle the two people in the harness would swing straight into the bridge rails. The wire would have to be vertical – and that meant hovering above the bridge. Cautiously he inched the 6-ton machine to the right, eyes darting to the radio altimeter to check he was above the safe height he had set himself. He was flying blind, for most of the ship's length was hidden from his view by the cabin floor. He was relying totally on Bill Campbell in the doorway giving him a running word-picture on the relative positions of ship and aircraft.

At last he reported that the winch cable was plumb – but at that moment a huge wave engulfed *Finneagle*. She staggered and rolled, dipping her port scuppers beneath the water. Her

143

mainmast arced sideways towards 'Rescue 38' like a toppling
tree.

'Up! Up! Up!' Campbell roared into the intercom. The
spar was only feet away from the rotor and still coming. One
touch against the blades and the Sea King would tear herself
apart, killing her crew and the Swedes waiting below. The
two Gnome engines howled. The machine reared upwards as
Lakey and Simpson hauled back on the controls. The slack,
curving cable sprang bow-string taut. With a savage force
the two people in the harness were yanked off the bridge
into mid-air. So abrupt was their ascent that they found
themselves dancing on the end of the cable in bare feet,
having left two pairs of clogs standing on deck!

Campbell winched in fast to dampen down the murderous
swing. As the survivors reeled in towards him he saw they
were women, white with fear, spinning face to face in the
twin harness. He was astonished to see that each had a young
boy clasped in her arms: small, frightened faces upturned to
the deafening roar of the helicopter, blond fringes plastered
flat by the rotor's downdraught.

'My God – they've got a kid each!' he gasped into the
microphone and immediately slowed the winch to its slowest
speed. It would be all too easy for a sudden movement
of the aircraft to dislodge one or both youngsters from
the women's precarious grasp. There would be no second
chance. A small child would die instantly in those raging seas.
Campbell seemed to hold his breath for a long time until the
human cargo rose level with the door. He and Bragg pulled
them aboard.

Once aboard, the boys' fear evaporated. Aged six and
three, they looked around them with bright-eyed excitement. First a shipwreck and now a ride in a helicopter –
what an adventure to recount to their friends back home in
Gothenburg.

Four saved on the first lift! It was an achievement that
augured well, though it soon transpired that the spectacular
method of their leaving the ship had caused a new problem.
When Campbell had managed to trail the high-line on to
Finneagle's bridge one of the sailors, in the manner of

seamen the world over when handed a rope, had hitched it to a stanchion. The sudden jerk had snapped it like a piece of cotton, breaking it at a weak point specifically built in as a fail-safe to prevent rescue helicopters being tethered and dragged out of the sky. Now they had only two high-lines left. While Bragg and Campbell attached one of them, Lakey jockeyed back to his original position in front of the ship's prow. This time the Swedes caught it on the first attempt and began to haul in the strop.

'Someone's using his loaf down there,' Campbell said approvingly. 'They've put the next two blokes *outside* the bridge rails so we can pull them straight off without dragging them into the rails.' For the pilots it was good news. It meant they could lift from the port flank without having to move inboard, risking another collision with the mainmast.

Of course, the two men would have a bit of a wild ride for they would swing outboard the moment they broke contact with the ship. But if their mates did the right thing and paid out the high-line until the wire was hanging more or less vertical, it shouldn't be too uncomfortable – certainly nothing like the violence of the first lift. In the eerie glow of the flames the two Swedes let go their grip on the bridge rails. They wheeled outwards across the confusion of torn water and driving spray.

Sergeant Bragg swore to himself. *Damn these sailors and their bloody knots*. Once more the high-line had been lashed to a stanchion. As the men swung out, it tautened suddenly – and broke. Campbell winched in at top speed – 200 feet per minute – lifting the men before the pendulum effect swung them back into the side of the bridge. They were dragged aboard and another high-line was attached to the cable.

This was the last one. If it, too, snapped there wouldn't be much hope of rescue for the 16 remaining seamen. Yet that, only moments later, is what almost happened.

As the men on *Finneagle's* bridge seized the line, their ship turned capriciously without warning, sheering violently to starboard and staggering under thousands of tons of water as her port side was presented to the oncoming sea. Desperate to keep the line slack, Lakey turned with the ship, reefing the

Sea King hard over to the right. But now the ship's captain was correcting his rudder and *Finneagle* drifted out of the pilot's sight beneath the aircraft's belly.

'Hey boss, it's a bit bloody warm back here!' Bragg's voice sounded a gentle warning. They were right over the fire!

As quickly as he could, for he was still conscious that they were down to their very last high-line, Lakey ruddered back to his original position by the port wing of the bridge. Even there the inferno was uncomfortably close. Fresh detonations sent flames, debris and oily black smoke mushrooming upwards, far above the helicopter. One explosion seemed to gather itself in the ship's bowels before erupting like a bursting blast furnace. The Sea King rolled wildly in the shock waves.

'Are you OK, Rescue 38?' came an anxious radio message from the Nimrod that was circling overhead.

'Yes, thanks, we're fine.'

'Thank Christ for that. We thought you'd blown up.'

At last the Swedish sailors had realized it was not a good idea to lash the high-line to the ship. Now they were using it properly, paying it out or even letting go altogether if they thought too much strain was about to be placed upon it.

Two by two they came up, crowding into the overladen cabin. It took an hour; 60 interminable, fearful, exhausting minutes, but at last the toiling airmen had 20 souls aboard. Only two remained on the ship – Captain Waenerlund and his chief engineer.

The former could not be seen; he was still at his post in the wheelhouse. The latter was on the wing of the bridge. He grabbed the high-line as it was lowered for the last time. He shrugged his way into the harness and then, using the meat cleaver with which he had felled the radio mast, banged loudly on the wheelhouse roof to signal.

Lakey recalls: 'The skipper came dashing out like a rat up a drainpipe and dived into the other harness. Bill hit the switch and he and the engineer swung outwards – though without anyone on the line it was a bit of a hairy ride for them, I'm afraid.'

The two officers were catapulted from the bridge, tumbling like circus artists through the screaming wind and the flame-lit night. It was a spectacular finale to a spectacular rescue.

There was a clamour of excited approval from *Finneagle's* crew as their last two shipmates swung in through the door. Rick Bragg sniffed. 'That's another bloody high-line gone for a ball of chalk,' he muttered. 'I wouldn't mind but I signed for 'em.'

The following July, Flight Lieutenant Lakey travelled to Buckingham Palace to receive the George Medal from the Queen for what his commanding officer had described as 'probably the most remarkable rescue in the history of the helicopter service anywhere in the world'.

Flight Lieutenant Campbell was decorated with the Air Force Cross. Sergeant Bragg received the Air Force Medal. Flight Lieutenant Simpson was presented with the Queen's Commendation for Valuable Service in the Air and a Queen's Commendation for Brave Conduct went to Squadron Leader Hamish Grant, the medical officer.

Other honours followed. Lakey received the Order of the Golden Lion of Stockholm and went to Los Angeles to be presented with the International Helicopter Heroism Award. He was elected 'Scot of the Year'. The crew became recipients of a new air-sea rescue award from the Fishermen and Mariners' Protection Society. *Finneagle's* owners sent them a cheque for £1,000 which they promptly donated to the RAF Benevolent Fund.

In Sweden, Lakey was fêted as a national hero. He flew there to be presented with the silver medal of the Swedish Lifesaving Association and to be reunited with *Finneagle's* crew, including three-year-old Jonas Gustavson and his six-year-old brother Johan. For four days he was an honoured guest at official functions. He was even able to board *Finneagle*, salvaged when the fire had been put out 10 days after the rescue, then being rebuilt in dry dock in Gothenburg. The owners presented him with a replica of her ship's bell, which now hangs in the Officers' Mess at RAF Lossiemouth.

Engraved on it are these words:

The crew members, their families and the owners of Finneagle *express their gratitude for the most courageous rescue of all on board the vessel when she was burning and in a gale and had to be abandoned at 3.10 on October 2, 1980.*

The bravery and endurance of the crew are beyond all praise.

11

John Spencer –
Diving into Darkness

For the two-man crew of the long, wallowing barge it was a queasy and uncomfortable voyage through the grey waters of the Solent. A spanking breeze had brought a chill to the air and was piling the seas into a short, steep-sided chop peaking 6 feet high and more. Dragging mutinously on the thick steel tow-line astern of the tug, the barge corkscrewed uneasily.

With his feet braced wide apart to keep his balance on the rearing deck of the wheelhouse, helmsman John Henderson flicked the wheel first one way, then the other, striving to keep the hawser straight and taut between the two vessels.

Below, in the bijou-sized galley, 40-year-old Steve Devereux fielded sliding pots and pans as he set about rustling up a scratch hot lunch for himself and his mate. No easy job. The scow drew so little draught she would have rolled on a wet sponge, he reckoned. Now, negotiating the narrow channel between the Hampshire coast and the Isle of Wight, waters notorious for being confused by crosscurrents, she reeled about like a gin-sodden crone on a seaside outing.

It was a little after 11 a.m. on Friday, 10 October 1980. Her tug, *Craigleath*, was just entering the narrowest part of the Solent, the half-mile wide bottleneck between the Hurst Castle peninsular and the Isle of Wight's Colwell Bay. As the barge trailed in her wake, John Henderson was working hard, glowing despite the cold, to keep her straight in the unpredictable seas. He grinned at the crash of crockery below and the awful, sulphurous language that drifted up from

149

Devereux's galley. He wound on more helm to keep station behind *Craigleath*, but a maverick wave pattern continued to shoulder his bows sideways. *You old bitch!* She was sluggish as hell, wilfully rolling off at a tangent from the tug's course so that the tow-line slackened and dipped into the sea.

He fought to bring her head round, but *Craigleath's* progress quickly snatched up the slack. Reverberating like a giant bowstring, the shivering, dripping hawser snapped bar-taut out of the water. The barge was still several points off course and the jerk against her bows made her heel savagely. She began to crab awkwardly through the water with waves breaking clear over her dipped rails. Yet still she refused to answer to her rudder.

The pull of the tow-line was remorseless. The list grew more pronounced and a horrified John Henderson found himself beginning to slip down deckplates that were inexorably turning into a wall. He cried to his mate in the galley: 'Steve! Out of there, for God's sake. She's going over. I can't hold her.'

But by then it was too late. A bewildered and fearful Henderson felt himself fall through the wheelhouse door, pitching painfully over the rail and sliding into the numbing cold of the Solent. Fighting for air and choking on brine, he surfaced in time to witness the closing moments of the catastrophe as the barge rolled slowly on to her back like a dying iron whale. He shouted, desperately, calling his friend's name as he trod water. But there was no reply, only the thunder of wave . . .

In the galley, deafened by the crash of upturning pans and splintering crockery, wildly disorientated by the compartment's steady rotation through 180 degree, Steve Devereux grabbed for something to hold on to, found nothing and slid helplessly downwards into a mess of spilled food, cooking utensils and shards of pottery and glass. He struggled to find his equilibrium, his brain, for the moment, unable to accept the evidence of his eye – the fact that the compartment was upside down; that the deckhead light which, only seconds before, had been above his head was now beneath his feet.

Even as he looked at it, the bulb dimmed and flickered out, plunging the galley into total darkness.

Then, with a terrifying roar, the water burst in . . .

*   *   *

The call for help to the search and rescue unit came at 11.20 a.m. on Channel Zero, the Coastguards' radio frequency. Lieutenant Bill Sample, RN, and his two-man Wessex crew of the search and rescue unit at HMS *Daedalus,* Lee-on-Solent, were waiting as the groundcrew pumped aviation kerosene into the underfloor fuel tanks to replace the 800 pounds they had just burned up on a routine training flight. Ian Weston, a petty officer, sat at the radio and radar complex in the aftercabin. Behind him, leaning out of the starboard door to ensure no one walked into the whirling 9-foot disc of the tail rotor, was the baby of the crew – 24-year-old Acting Leading Aircrewman John Spencer. In the perspex canopy, set on the Wessex's bulbous snout, Lieutenant Sample lounged in the right-hand pilot's seat, keeping the two Gnome jets burning and turning.

Barge under tow has overturned off Hurst Castle near the Needles, was the Coastguard's message. *Two men believed to be in the water. Urgently request an SAR helicopter search.*

As refuelling finished, Sample opened his throttles. Within seconds the Wessex had lifted itself off the wet tarmac and was clopping along at a brisk 130 miles per hour for the Needles.

In the cabin John Spencer listened intently and nervously to updated radio reports – one man had been rescued from the sea by the tug's crew. The other was believed trapped, hopefully surviving in a pocket of air inside the overturned barge.

'What made me nervous was the realization that I was about to face my first diving rescue,' he said later. 'I'd done one winch rescue before and, of course, had completed diving training, but this was to be the first time I would have to dive for real.'

151

Eleven minutes and 17 miles later the helicopter was hanging in the gusty breeze above the whaleback hump of the barge's keel. Standing there, waving frantically to the rescue machine, was a member of *Craigleath's* crew. John Spencer waited apprehensively in the doorway trussed in his wet suit and BASAR (breathing apparatus search and rescue), alert for the signal that would send him plunging into the muddy churning waters 15 feet below.

'Permission to despatch the driver, sir?' Petty Officer Weston asked the formal question over the intercom with punctilious correctness. The reply was in the affirmative and he tapped Spencer twice on the shoulder. The young diver took a deep breath and jumped.

The icy shock came like a physical blow as he plunged beneath the waves. He sucked in a lungful of rubbery oxygen and kicked for the surface. As he swam for the barge he heard the clamour of the helicopter retreating in the distance. (Later he discovered it had returned to *Daedalus* to collect more divers.) His hands touched the chill metal of the barge and he shouted to the tug-man standing there: 'Where is he, then?'

'In the accommodation compartment,' came the reply. 'We can hear him knocking on the hull.'

'How do I get in?'

'The entrance is on the starboard side – back towards the stern somewhere.'

Spencer acknowledged with a wave, ducked beneath the waves – and immediately found himself almost blind. The storm had stirred up so much muck from the sea bed that he could see no further than a foot in front of his face mask. Largely by feel, he began to make his way down the starboard side until his hands were able to grasp the gunwale rails. He ducked underneath them and groped his way towards the inverted superstructure below the stern.

He touched his finger ends along weld seams and rivet heads, searching for a door or hatch, an opening of any sort that might lead him to the trapped wretch inside. Soon his outstretched hands encountered a gap and traced its outline. It was a doorway. Slowly and with mounting apprehension he swam inside. Instantly, the meagre glimmer of light there had been outside vanished, snuffed out as though by a light switch. Not a glimmer relieved a blackness that was so impenetrable it seemed solid.

For long, uncertain moments he hung still in the water, forcing himself to summon up the courage to explore further into the unknown. He made a conscious effort to slow his breathing to a slow, steady rhythm – panicky gasps would only empty his air bottles more quickly.

Come on, Spence – this is for real. There's some poor sod stuck in there waiting for you.

He finned his way into the compartment, slowly waving his hands in front of him like the antennae of some blind creature from the sea bed. He began to swim upwards. His fingers brushed against something cold and oval-shaped that was hanging down from the upturned deck. He scrabbled at it, totally mystified. Then he pushed his head forward until his eyes were a couple of inches away, but it was no good, he still couldn't see a damned thing. He grinned weakly to himself as he finally identified the mystery object by touch. It was a WC bowl; obviously he was in the heads. There would, he reasoned, be only one entrance – the one he had come through – so further exploration was unnecessary.

Unseeing, he felt his way back outside. Hand over hand he fended himself across the front of the bridge superstructure to explore the port side – and was suddenly swearing and fighting to free himself as he blundered into a tangle of ropes hanging like vines from the deck. He hacked himself free with his aircrew knife.

The search of the port side proved fruitless. Though he tracked back and forth for several minutes he found no opening. Disappointed and acutely conscious that time was precious, he struggled back through the spaghetti-mess of ropes to the starboard side. This time he ignored the entrance to the heads and kept going, angling round the corner of the superstructure until he was by the rear bulkhead of the bridge.

There, almost immediately, he discovered a door and swam through, back once more in a world totally without light. His hand bumped against something which he grabbed and identified as the ship's wheel. That was better. Surely there must be a companion-way from the wheelhouse to the cramped living accommodation; it could be only a matter of time before he discovered it.

Talking of time . . . he peered at the luminous dial of his waterproof watch and noted with astonishment that he had been under water for half an hour. 'Although I'd tried to control my breathing, being scared I had obviously used more than I thought I had because I'd already emptied one cylinder. So I decided to go back to the surface to get a new supply.'

He swam back into blessed daylight, heartened to see that the Wessex had returned, bringing fresh air bottles and two more divers, now standing on the hull beside the seaman from *Craigleath*. He recognized them as Chief Aircrewman Dave 'Bomber' Brown, head of Spencer's section, and Chris Crossley, another trained diver. They dragged him on to the hull.

'Do you want me to go down with you, Spence?' Brown asked, as the young diver shrugged his way into the straps of a new brace of oxygen bottles.

'No, I've begun to find my way round a bit – but I do want a word with this civvie to see if he can help me find a way in. It's as black as buggery down there.'

He explained to the *Craigleath* man that he had found the entrance to the wheelhouse and received the welcome news that the door to the accommodation section was right next to it. He jumped back into the water and quickly found what he was seeking. But it was jammed shut, locked by metal clips which refused to budge when he tried to turn them. They might just as well have been welded in place. He tried again, fighting against the drag of a strong current that was pushing him from the door. The result was the same.

Nothing's easy, is it? He swam back to the surface and called for a hammer. Brown passed him a mallet, then said, 'Here, Spence, take this as well and tie it to the door. It'll be a guide for us if we have to come after you.' The diver took the rope end the Chief had proffered and submerged once more.

Back at the door he hitched the rope to the handle and, kicking hard with his flippers to counter the drag of the current, swung the mallet in a slow-motion thump against the metal clip. It didn't budge a millimetre. He took a harder swing, then another and another, gritting his teeth and breathing hard on his precious oxygen supply. For three minutes, four, five, he battered at the stubborn clip. Hot sweat trickled down inside the wet suit. But slowly the locking device was moving, turning almost imperceptibly with each echoing blow.

With a muffled clang it shifted, then Spencer was wrestling with the ponderous steel door, struggling to open it against the heavy press of the current. He gave a mighty heave and slammed it back against the wall. With a return of his earlier feelings of foreboding, his mind busy with disturbing images of being lost or trapped inside the sinking hulk, he floated in through the doorway, still gasping from his exertions.

'I had really serious doubts about going ahead,' he admitted to me afterwards. 'Somehow it seemed even more black than before. I felt my way in and could see absolutely nothing. It was just as if someone had put my eyes out. I was scared – really scared. I had no idea which way to go or what lay ahead. The one thought that kept coming back to me was that once I got inside I wouldn't be able to find my way out again. I made myself take a few slow, deep breaths and remember saying to myself, *Look, you shouldn't be working as a diver if you're not up to it.*

'That helped a bit. So I went in a few more feet and let myself begin to drift upwards.'

It took almost every ounce of willpower he possessed, and much courage besides, to enter that black and fearsome chamber. His heart thudded as he began rising slowly towards the compartment's deck through a tangle of unidentifiable jetsam that bumped and moved through the black water as the doomed barge stirred in the waves and current. After what seemed like an hour or two, but was probably only a few minutes, he felt his hands growing warm. Why, he wondered, should one layer of water be warmer than another?

155

Of course! The answer was simple; his hands were no longer in water – they were reaching out into the pocket of trapped air. He rose another couple of feet and felt his head break the surface. Somehow he had expected to be able to see something, if only the dimmest loom of light once he was out of the water. But though he trod water, turning himself through a full 360 degrees, the oppressive blackness was still unremitting. It pressed down on him with an almost physical force.

But he was still able to hear. As he swallowed hard to relieve the pressure on his eardrums the sound came to him – an eerie mumbling, occasionally broken by the soft, wretched sobbing of a man who has been pushed close to the limits of human endurance.

With his own fear abating, if only slightly, the diver felt a stab of pity for the terror-stricken sailor clinging on to life in that black pocket. God alone knew what horrors he had lived through since the barge had turned turtle. Small wonder that he whimpered to himself in what seemed certain to become his tomb.

When Spencer spoke his voice was low and soothing, as though speaking to a hurt child. For he was fearful that the shock of hearing another human would cause Devereux to fling himself through the water, barging him away from the one spot he knew was directly above the route to safety, maybe injuring or even drowning him in his panic.

'Hello, mate. You're going to be all right. No – don't move. Stay where you are and listen to what I say . . .' His words echoed softly in the confines of the galley.

Willing the man to remain still he explained the situation, realizing as he spoke that what he was about to say would test the other's courage, perhaps beyond what could be expected of anyone. For if there was to be any chance of saving him, he would have to leave him alone to his nightmare yet again. Though the descent to the door was a comparatively short one it would seem like an eternity in that blackness to a frightened man with only one lungful of air to keep him going. Any delay – a wrong turn or obstruction – would bring panic. Almost certainly that would be fatal for Devereux and, caught in the clutches of a drowning man, probably for Spencer himself.

'. . . so I'm going to have to go back up top and get you a set of breathing apparatus,' he went on. 'I'll be right back. Just a few minutes, that's all – I promise you.'

There was a long silence as Devereux weighed his words. First he had known despair, the near certainty of a miserable, choking death. Then hope had come. Now, for a time, that hope was to be snatched away. In that time the air pocket could exhaust itself, or the barge sink.

It was a moment of crushing disappointment. But with only his head and shoulders clear of the water in the finite reservoir of air, Steve Devereux discovered his own brand of courage.

'Yes – I'll wait,' he said, his voice husky but steady now. 'For Christ's sake be as quick as you can. The water's rising all the time. It won't last long.'

'I'll be back in a jiffy,' Spencer answered with a breezy reassurance he didn't feel, for it was plain the barge was gradually settling deeper in the water. He ducked down. His downward swim seemed to last for ever, but at last there was a feeble hint of murky light ahead. He finned through the doorway and up to the surface.

'I've found him!' he gasped to 'Bomber' Brown. 'But he needs a breathing set – that's the only way I'm going to get him out. Can you give us a hand? There's not room for two of us in there, but you could follow me in and pass the spare set to me.'

Without a word Brown tucked a BASAR under his arm and slid off the hull into the water. Spencer led the way, grateful for the older man's foresight in suggesting that he should tie a rope to the door as a guideline. For it led them straight to their goal. Spencer led the way, striking upwards through the blackness with Brown hanging on to his leg. When his head broke clear of the water he felt downwards with his left arm, grasping the BASAR that the chief petty officer passed up to him from his position beneath Spencer's flippers. There was an audible gasp of relief when the diver spoke. 'Told you I wouldn't hang about, mate. Now I've got a breathing set for you. What I want you to do is come slowly towards me. I'll keep talking and you come towards the sound . . . but slowly, mind you.' He felt the movement in the water as the man forged towards him.

'Everything's switched on and ready for you. I've got the mouthpiece in my hand; all you've got to do is feel for it and stick it between your teeth.'

A cold hand fastened over his own and the mouthpiece was plucked from his grasp. A moment later he heard the rhythmic in-out hissing as Devereux began to take air. By feel and guesswork he helped thread the harness over the other's shoulders. There was an eruption in the water beside him as 'Bomber' Brown surfaced. 'Hurry up, Spence,' he urged. 'Let's sod off quickly. I'll grab his legs and pull him down; you follow us.

'By the way,' he added conversationally, 'I hope you know you've been standing on my bloody head for the last 10 minutes.'

Spencer forced himself to wait in that claustrophobic dark-ness as his two companions sank beneath the surface, willing himself to remain still until he estimated they had reached the door. Only then, and with a profound sense of relief, did he begin to follow.

But his head was barely submerged before he found him-self in trouble. Something was blocking his path. *For Christ's sake* . . . He forced his way past it, only to be fetched up short again as he entangled himself with the rungs of a ladder floating with the other debris. He seemed to be surrounded by nameless objects that were bumping against him, impeding him, trying to trap him, holding him there until the barge sank to the sea bed. He cursed and sweated, thrashing and kicking in a sea of absolute darkness as the rising tide of panic threatened to engulf him.

Then training took over – the textbooks, the lectures and the practice dives. Most of all, the discipline. 'Bomber' he knew, would never leave him. He stopped struggling and surfaced again in the air pocket, removing his mouthpiece to conserve his oxygen supply. He bobbed about sightlessly among the debris and, after two or three minutes, one leg appeared to be free of obstructions.

He slipped his mouthpiece back in place and ducked under the surface for the second time. The underwater rubbish dump was still there, but now the barrier seemed less impenetrable. Ignoring the bumps and scrapes against his legs and arms, he forced his way downwards. Suddenly the water was unobstructed and he was swimming with all his strength towards the wonderful, murky rectangle of light that was his road to salvation.

His head bobbed clear of the Solent just in time to see the Wessex winching the man he had saved out of the waves for the short flight to the nearest Royal Navy hospital. 'Bomber' Brown beamed encouragingly as he trod water beside the settling barge, trying to squeeze the air out of the lifejacket he had inflated in order to speed the progress of Devereux and himself to the surface.

'Good to see you, Spence,' he called. 'Well done lad, well done.'

John Spencer grinned back, suddenly proud of their achievement. Then he turned and dived again; he had one more task to complete. When he had freed the clips on the door, he had jammed the mallet behind one of the hinges for safe-keeping; the guide rope was still lashed to the door handle – both signed-for articles on the Wessex's inventory. He'd be damned if he would leave them where they were. Somehow, after all the dramas of that morning, he couldn't bring himself to mess about completing all the official bumf that would be necessary to write them off . . .

Soon after the epic rescue that freed Steve Devereux after 105 minutes of purgatory, other paperwork was working its way through the Navy's official channels. Marked 'Staff in Confidence', it was a citation chronicling Spencer's extraordinary heroism. In July 1981 he found himself lined up with other heroes at Buckingham Palace, waiting to receive the Queen's Gallantry Medal.

A little more than a year later he was back at the Palace, this time to receive a bar to his QGM and thus become the first member of the Royal Navy to be so honoured twice.

It was awarded for his rescue, by helicopter winch, of an 18-month-old baby, a woman and two deck hands from a badly listing ship in appalling storms off Portland Bill on 13 December 1981.

Once again John Spencer had known the grip of fear; once again at great personal risk he had overcome that fear to do his duty in the very highest traditions of his Service.

12

Alasdair Campbell – Amateurs to the Rescue

The trawler *Elinor Viking*, an 86-footer from Aberdeen, was being brutally beaten to pieces, torn apart by the sheer force of the elements assaulting her in the heart of a powerful gale. The crashes and screams of her slow annihilation sounded a booming counterpoint to the thunder of the breaking seas. Overlaying it all was the near-deafening clatter of the red, white and blue helicopter that hovered overhead.

In all this din, the voices of the two men on the trawler's deck were lost, even though their faces were only inches apart as they yelled angry abuse at each other, staggering to keep their balance, grabbing stanchions for support, as breaking waves constantly burst over them.

Both were over 6 feet tall. Both were aware that it could be only a matter of minutes before the foundering fishing vessel broke her back over the fulcrum of a granite reef. Both Celts and stubborn, each refused to give way in an argument that was quickly escalating towards a brawl.

One of them, cocooned in a rubber suit and aircrew crash helmet, was slightly taller than his antagonist. He was Alasdair Campbell, winchman of the helicopter. The other was the man he had come to rescue, Alex Flett, *Elinor Viking's* skipper. Mulishly, however, he declined to be rescued. His sense of duty would not permit him to abandon ship until the seven other men on board had been saved. He was the captain, he maintained, therefore he would be the last to leave. And there was an end to the matter.

Though exhausted and suffering badly from the deadly chill of hypothermia he was a powerful man – and a determined one. His big hands were locked round the guard rails and Campbell could not break his grip.

'Come on, you bloody fool,' the winchman bawled. 'Let go for Christ's sake!'

Flett shook his bowed head. 'Bugger off,' he gasped. 'I'm not shifting till you've taken the others. Come back for me when they're safe.'

It was an impasse and had been for several minutes.

Campbell, at one time a major in the Inniskilling Dragoon Guards, cursed the obstinate seaman bitterly and obscenely. In an instant, temper flared into sudden fury. He balled his right hand into a fist and drew it back . . .

*   *   *

Just over 100 miles north-east of John O'Groats, the tiny airport at Sumburgh perches on the very southernmost tip of the largest of the 100 islands that make up the Shetlands. From this, the remotest inhabited territory in the British Isles, no more than a series of rocky specks in the North Atlantic, you can travel north without seeing land until you reach the Polar icecap.

For centuries, the hardy Shetlanders lived a quiet, tough life on a handful of the barren and treeless islands, eking out a living from their crofts or fishing the tempestuous seas between Norway and Greenland.

Then, beneath those icy seas, oil was discovered. Almost overnight, the Shetlands were transformed beyond recognition. Oilmen flocked there from all over the globe, bringing with them that most versatile mode of transport, the helicopter.

Unlike the rest of the British coastline, the Shetlands lack close-at-hand coverage by the RAF and Royal Navy's search and rescue network; the already overstretched services cannot afford the men or machines to set up a base there. So British Airways, then one of the main contractors to the oil companies, decided to form their own rudimentary air-sea rescue service. It had barely reached an embryonic stage when, on the night of Friday, 9 December 1977 – untrained, unrehearsed and unprepared – it was put to the test in truly appalling conditions. Four men, civilian volunteers, pulled off what was later to be described by the coastguards as 'one of the most outstanding air evacuations in the history of lifesaving'.

And it was all the work of amateurs, magnificent amateurs.

*   *   *

To the west of the Shetlands, 3 miles off the whaleback island of Papa Stour, lies a place of dread for all mariners. The Ve Skerries is a jumble of underwater mountain peaks that jut out of deep waters. Over the centuries countless ships have ripped themselves apart on this devil's graveyard of rocks.

Shetlanders still tell the story and sing the lament of the *Ben Doran*, an Aberdeen trawler which ran aground there during a March storm in 1930. Her crew lashed themselves to the rigging and waited for help, knowing their plight had been seen from the shore. But the storm was so tumultuous that the islanders could not launch a boat for three days . . . three horrifying days during which they could only watch helplessly through telescopes and binoculars as, one by one, the trawlermen died of exposure. When a boat finally reached her, she was a ship of dead men. Not one had survived.

On the evening of 9 December 1977, the *Elinor Viking* was running for shelter on the west coast of Shetland when she found, not land, but those same Ve Skerries . . .

It was 5 p.m. and British Airways' operation at Sumburgh was winding down for the evening when chief pilot and deputy manager George Bain took the 'Mayday' call from Wick coastguard. He listened intently as the duty officer described the *Elinor Viking's* plight. Though totally without any air-sea rescue experience he immediately volunteered to help. Apart from himself there was only one other pilot still in the office, Campbell Bosanquet, a 30-year-old former RAF officer who had recently qualified as a BA captain. Bain explained the emergency and Bosanquet immediately agreed to accompany him on the mission.

Brian Johnstone, 36, one-time Royal Navy winchman, now a BA operations assistant, was watching television at his home 6 miles from the airfield when he received a terse telephone message from the operations room:

'Get your backside in gear and on your bike – we need you.'

Alasdair Campbell was muttering testily to himself as he struggled with the innards of his wife's broken washing machine in the garage of his home in the village of Tolob, close by the airfield boundary. He sighed as his wife Carole called him to the telephone. He listened without speaking as Bain explained matters to him.

Major Campbell was an experienced helicopter pilot, but it was not as a pilot that he was now being asked to help. He was needed as a winchman – while Johnstone, the more experienced man, operated the winch control and gave directions to the pilot. It was an unenviable role for a comparative novice but he did not hesitate. Two minutes later he, too, was heading for Sumburgh.

As Johnstone and Campbell raced down the narrow Shetland roads towards the airfield lights, mechanics were busy preparing one of the big Sikorsky S61 helicopters for a rescue mission – topping up her fuel tanks, removing 13 of her 20 passenger seats and rigging a gallows-like steel winch in the forward starboard doorway. At 5.10, with his crew aboard, George Bain fired the helicopter's two 1,500-horsepower General Electric jets.

As Alasdair Campbell struggled into his gear – woollen combinations, a rubber immersion suit welded to rubber boots and a toughened plastic helmet – he felt a flutter of apprehension. He knew nothing but the theory of search and rescue techniques. His only practical experience had been a couple of practice winchings since joining BA three years earlier. He began to wish he had taken more notice of what the instructor had said.

In the Captain's seat on the right-hand side of the flight deck George Bain frowned as he spotted a fault the mechanics had not had time to repair. The starboard landing light swivel mechanism had seized up; when lit, it would shine uselessly at an awkward angle to the left.

Bain grunted. 'Too late to do anything now. We'll just have to live with it.'

It was a decision that was to have dramatic consequences.

At 5.20 p.m. the helicopter – call sign Bravo Juliet – wallowed into the blustery night sky, turned ponderously in the gusting wind and clattered off on a north-westerly course for the Ve Skerries, 35 miles away.

It was a rough night. A Force 10 gale hammered in from the south-east at over 60 miles per hour, driving before it blinding squalls of rain. Flying at 125 miles per hour, Bravo Juliet skidded and bounced along in the black no man's between the 300-foot cloud base and the heaving white waters of the Atlantic.

Captain Bain had already been told by the Wick coastguard that the Aith lifeboat had been launched soon after the first 'Mayday' call. Now, as he headed for the search area, the pilot received further good news from two more radio messages. The first told him that a second S61 had been sent out by Sumburgh. Call sign Delta Alpha, she would act as back-up and radio relay aircraft. The second message, from the Northern Rescue Coordination Centre at Pitreavie Castle, near Edinburgh, announced that an RAF Nimrod reconaissance aircraft was en route to the Ve Skerries from a Strike Command base on the Scottish mainland.

As he digested these two welcome facts, George Bain saw a cluster of fireflies begin to loom out of the blackness and driving spray – the navigation lights of several vessels that had converged to offer assistance after picking up the 'Mayday' call.

Bain flew slowly over each set of lights. None was the *Elinor Viking* but in the distance the blackness was lit by the sudden red stain of a distress flare. 'Here we go,' he said jubilantly, opening his throttles and wheeling towards the guttering flame. A few minutes later he was circling over another ship. She was not the *Elinor Viking* either – but from her bridge a powerful searchlight stabbed a blue-white beam into the blackness.

It was a signpost. Slowly Bain nosed forward above the pencil of light, easing down to a height of 50 feet. He and his crew peered into the night, seeking the dying ship. Brian Johnstone, kneeling in the doorway, found the first clue. He sniffed deeply and spoke into his mike. 'I can smell diesel fuel. She must be round here somewhere.'

He had barely finished speaking when Campbell Bosanquet's voice came over the intercom: 'There she is – 100 metres on the port side.'

It was 6.20 p.m. Bain ruddered left and there she was . . . skewered on the cruel peak of the Skerries, her bows pointing east as if in a last futile lunge for the shelter of Papa Stour. Smothered in driving spray she was listing 50 degrees to starboard, staggering upright each time a wave punched into her flanks. When the waters retreated she would flop back on the rocks with a booming reverberation that was heard even above the thunder of the helicopter.

Time and again she vanished as rolling 15-foot waves exploded across her. Every time she lay over, the airmen caught sight of a dreadful mortal wound, a 9-foot gash in her underbelly where the rocks had eviscerated her.

Huddled on her port side, sheltering beneath the overhang of her bridge, was her crew. Often waist-deep in sluicing rivers of waters, they ducked as the sheer fury of the sea literally tore lumps off their ship, demolishing her piece by piece.

'Jesus – have you ever seen anything like it?' said an awestruck Johnstone.

The only man who could not hear him was Alasdair Campbell. As winchman, the tall major was not linked to the intercom. Bracing himself in the open doorway, he was alone with his private and very uncomfortable thoughts. Until Brian Johnstone had touched him on the shoulder and pointed to the winch hook, he had remained illogically convinced that it would somehow all turn out to be a mistake or a false alarm, that the trawlermen would give them a cheery thumbs-up and a wave so they could head back to the airport in time for tea.

Now as he fumbled to clip his harness to the hook, came the unpalatable realization that in a few seconds he must leave the comforting confines of the helicopter, swing into space and sink down the winch speed of 120 feet a minute into the cauldron. And with that realization came a nagging fear that the task was too demanding; that there was nothing he could do to help the eight sodden wretches clinging to the *Elinor Viking*; that his reserves of courage would fail him.

Yet without him they would die.

He clenched his teeth when the harness suddenly tightened round his waist and thighs as Brian Johnstone winched him up and out through the doorway. The powerful downdraught from the main rotor set him see-sawing on the end of the line, spinning and jinking, lower and lower towards the white fog of sea spray.

His life was literally in Johnstone's hands. The winch operator – the only member of the crew who could see Campbell – had become the pilot's eyes. Into his throat mike he called an unceasing stream of minor course corrections to try to put the winchman safely aboard. At the same time he was constantly winching in and out in a bid to keep Campbell steady, playing him as an angler will play a fish to prevent a sudden strain on the line.

Despite the cold – the temperature was only a few degrees above freezing – Johnstone sweated as he aimed his friend towards the obvious landing spot, a relatively wide expanse of deck, aft of the wheelhouse. His eyes, however, were fixed firmly on what he had already noted as a potential disaster area – two radio aerial wires stretched between the mainmast and the aftermast. If he inadvertently swung Campbell into one of those it would slice through the immersion suit – and the flesh below – like a grocer's cheese-cutter.

George Bain, too, was aware of the peril and was striving to hover steadily, thus giving Johnstone a chance to put Campbell down near the ship's rails, well clear of the wires. But like all helicopter pilots he needed a reference point on which to fix his eyes. Without one, he was like a motorist trying to drive at speed without lights down a foggy road that had neither cats' eyes nor white lines.

Yet all he could see was the *Elinor Viking*, rolling and pitching in her death throes. In attempting a steady hover and with no datum point, he inevitably began aping her movements, rolling the aircraft back and forth. On the end of the wire Alasdair Campbell began a sickening pendulum swing.

'Left! Left! Left!' The voice in George Bain's headset almost deafened him. It had come from Brian Johnstone. Concern for the winchman's predicament turned to sudden alarm as the ship snapped upright on a raising wave, flinging her stout steel aftermast and radio aerials towards the figure on the end of the wire.

Campbell swore as he saw them coming, instinctively reaching out to fend them off. He gasped with shock as his body thudded into the crosstree with painful force. There was a sharp tearing sound. In an instant, his inflatable lifejacket ripped apart on some unseen projection. God help him now if he had to swim for it . . .

Almost immediately there was a vicious jerk and his scrabbling fingers were yanked free of the mast as he was swung backwards over the open sea. He was bruised and apprehensive, his Mae West lifejacket was useless, but some-how he had escaped serious injury. He felt himself rising fast as Johnstone hit the winch switch at top speed. Hands reached out for him, pulling him into the cabin. There was a hasty shouted conference with the winch operator. 'I'm OK,' he told him. 'Really, I mean it. Put me back down again and I'll have another crack at it . . . but not near that bloody mast for Pete's sake!' 'All right, if you're sure,' Johnstone replied, relieved that his friend was unhurt. 'How about giving it a crack on that square of deck on the port side of the bridge?'

The spot he indicated was horribly small, 3 or 4 feet square at most, but had the advantage of being bounded on one side by the shelter of the bridge and on the other by the handholds the ship's rails afforded.

Campbell nodded.

Pirouetting on the end of the wire, his outstretched fingers just brushing those of the fishermen reaching up for him he was almost home, if not dry, when disaster threatened again.

A huge wave, swollen with thousands of tons of water, cascaded into *Elinor Viking's* starboard flank, flinging her bodily upwards. The main mast swung sideways – straight towards the whirling rotor blades. One touch and they would shear. The 9-ton machine would fall out of the sky and crash on deck. Both crews would die instantly.

Pure instinct made George Bain haul back on the controls. With engines screaming the big helicopter reared upwards, avoiding destruction by inches. Flying through the night in wild, confused arcs, jerking sickeningly on the end of the wire, Alasdair Campbell was bewildered and helpless. All he could do was give vent with an unending stream of curses. Somehow it seemed to help.

Nearly 4,000 feet above the drama, the second helicopter Delta Alpha was circling, relaying messages through an incredibly complicated and cumbersome lash-up of communication links. Though by now the Aith lifeboat was almost in sight, Captain Bain was unable to talk with her coxswain, Kenny Henry. Instead he radioed messages to Delta Alpha, the back-up helicopter, whose captain passed him to Sumburgh. From there the duty controller phoned Lerwick coastguards who, in turn, relayed the information to a radio-equipped Land Rover parked on high ground. From this vehicle it was radioed to Aith coastguard who alone could speak to the lifeboat.

Bravo Juliet was unable to communicate because her low altitude limited her radio range. The same factor made it almost impossible for the RAF Nimrod – now circling high overhead – to pinpoint the whereabouts of the helicopter; its radar could not single her out from the 'mush' of confused echoes by the breaking waves.

But as the four BA men recovered from the shock of near-disaster, copilot Bosanquet hit on an ingenious method of guiding the big patrol plane towards them. When Bain headed once more towards the wreck, the young second pilot switched on the SARBE (search and rescue beacon) that was clipped to his lifejacket. It began emitting a constant series of radio signals. The ruse worked like a charm. Seconds later the Nimrod had pinpointed them and was turning for a run-in to drop illuminating flares.

At the same time the helicopter crew learned another trick. As they steadied in the hover in just the right place to put Alasdair Campbell on target, Bosanquet noted a curious coincidence. The cross-eyed starboard landing light had settled on the only object visible in the shifting, confused seascape – a small rock forward and to the left of the helicopter's nose. The port one was shining forward and down on *Elinor Viking*'s deck.

That was it! Far from being the liability the crew had expected, the faulty light had turned out to be a godsend. Purely by accident they had found the vital datum point they so desperately needed in order to hover steadily. The notion was simple, but it worked. As long as they kept one light on the rock and the other on the trawler, they were in the right position.

Three minutes later Alasdair Campbell's boots thudded on to the pocket handkerchief square of deck between the wheelhouse and the port rails. Dead on cue, the first of the Nimrod's flares burst through the angry storm clouds, casting the awesome scene into brilliant, eerie relief. In the eye-aching glare the airmen saw for the first time the reality of *Elinor Viking*'s death agonies as the night rang with the sounds of her destruction and the torn blue and white hull was slowly disembowelled on the sharp rocks. Thirty seconds later the flare died away and the tableau faded into blackness once more.

Alasdair Campbell clung to the ship's rails as waves avalanched across him. The deck thrust up dizzily beneath his feet, only to drop away moments later as the keel smashed back on the rocks with a force that jarred every bone in his body. It was, he said later, like being in a car crash every few seconds. God knows what it must have been like for the trawlermen who had been suffering this dreadful punishment for the last two hours.

Thirty feet above, kneeling in the helicopters's doorway, Brian Johnstone made constant small movements of the winch control. The idea was to give Campbell enough cable to allow him complete freedom of movement, but not so much that he would get caught in a tangle of spare wire.

Blinking spray from his eyes, the winchman beckoned to the knot of sailors sheltering beneath the sloping bridge overhang. One man slithered towards him, selected by skipper Flett who had long before ordained the pecking order in which his crew would abandon ship, should the opportunity present itself.

Fighting for balance as a waist-high wall of water swept the deck, the winchman made a grab for the man and struggled to slip the lifting strop over his head and shoulders. It seemed an age before it was in position, but finally Campbell gave a thumbs' up sign to Johnstone.

Once again the sea perversely chose a crucial moment to take a hand. A particularly heavy swell rolled across the small rock that was the pilot's datum point, swamping it. Instantly they were disorientated and involuntarily over-corrected on the controls. The S61 drifted forward, carrying the two men towards the bridge overhang. Johnstone bawled a warning, ramming the winch switch upwards. If he could not lift them out in time and they jammed beneath the bridge, the cable to which they were hooked would rip them into pieces. Captain Bain hauled back on his stick. With stomach-churning force the pair on the wire were yanked clear of danger and swung clear over the rails. It was a ghastly, wild ride, but they were safe once more.

Two minutes later the survivor was in the cabin and a triumphantly grinning Alasdair Campbell was on his way back down for the next man. Twice more he made that perilous descent, each time gaining in confidence and experience, each time bringing up a cold and shivering trawlerman.

For the fourth time he touched on the deck and made a grab for the rails. 'Come on – who's next?' he bawled.

That was when the argument started.

Captain Flett was in a poor way. Much earlier he had bravely handed his own protective clothing to another crew member. Dressed only in trousers, sweater and a pair of old carpet slippers he had constantly waded through freezing water below deck to operate the radio. Now he was almost all-in.

His crew insisted he should now be lifted off, but Flett, literally dying on his feet, refused to compromise his flinty sense of duty. He was the skipper; he would leave when, and only when, every member of his ship's company had been saved, and not a moment sooner.

Campbell begged, reasoned and pleaded but the Aberdonian clung steadfastly to the rails, shaking his head obdurately. The winchman swore and roared at him. Still to no avail.

So Campbell hit him.

'I gave him a tremendous clout in the face with my fist,' Campbell recalls. 'He staggered back and his glasses flew off . . . but the shock made him let go of the rails.'

Fury pumped adrenalin into weary muscles. The skipper bellowed with rage and raised his fists. It was just what Campbell wanted. Adroitly, he slipped the stoop over Flett's head and shoulders and signalled wildly to Brian Johnstone, gesturing upwards with both arms.

Cursing and struggling the two were whisked up in the air towards the open door. Inside the cabin the trawlerman glowered at the winchman. 'You bastard,' he cursed bitterly. 'You've made me lose me glasses. Brand new they were too.'

But then the fight went out of him and he slumped down on the floor, his body trembling with shock and cold. Only guts and his sense of responsibility had kept him going for the last two hours.

'Just get my lads off, will you?' he pleaded. Campbell nodded.

At that moment heartening news came over the complex communications link . . . Coxswain Kenny Henry had arrived with the Aith lifeboat to take off the remainder of *Elinor Viking*'s crew. Soon the helicopter crew could pick her out, crashing sturdily through the breaking seas towards the Ve Skerries.

Henry's skill and courage at the helm of the lifeboat were renowned throughout the Shetlands. His crew were seasoned sailors. The untrained flyers felt a surge of relief that at last they could hand over their perilous task to the experts.

That relief was short-lived. The lifeboat tacked up and down the *Elinor Viking*'s flank a few times while the RNLI men studied her and the rocks. Then came another message, relayed via Delta Alpha: 'Aith lifeboat report they cannot get close enough to the casualty because of the rocks. It's up to you Bravo Juliet.'

Amateur night, after all, would have to continue; once more the big helicopter clopped back into position above the dying ship. The pilots steered until the landing lights were shining once again on the little rock and the deck. Alasdair Campbell swung out into space yet again and watched the little square of deck rise up towards him. Four rescued; four to go . . .

One by one the survivors were lifted. Experience made each operation slightly easier than the last; and each success-ful rescue sent the helicopter crew's morale soaring to new heights.

Finally only one man remained on deck, Charlie Cussiter, the mate. As second-in-command he had maintained the proud seafaring tradition his skipper had been denied – that of staying with the ship until the last.

As the winch cable whisked him and Major Campbell into space the two men looked down at the scene of destruction below. With one accord they both raised their fingers in a 'V' sign – a sailor's and a soldier's farewell to the ship that had almost killed them both. Then they grinned sheepishly at each other.

The flight home, into the teeth of blustering headwinds, was long and tedious, but uneventful. Campbell and John-stone busied themselves in the cabin making the trawlermen comfortable – particularly Alex Frett who, unconscious and in deep shock, was hovering close to death. Doctors later estimated that without treatment he would have died within an hour or so.

173

And *Elinor Viking*? She sank, little more than a quarter of an hour after Charlie Cussiter was winched to safety.

At 8.30 p.m. with only 30 minutes of fuel remaining in her tanks, Bravo Juliet touched down at Sumburgh Airport where a fleet of ambulances waited to take the survivors to hospital. The helicopter crew watched as the casualties were loaded aboard and then, almost drunk with euphoria at having pulled off a rescue which from the start had appeared impossible, made tracks for the British Airways clubhouse bar beside the airfield. There they were joined by the crew of Delta Alpha, the back-up helicopter, and the men from the operations room. The ensuing thrash lasted long into the wee small hours of the morning . . .

Honours followed thick and fast on the heels of this remarkable rescue. No fewer than 17 individual and collective ones were awarded. The crew became the first-ever recipients of the Prince Philip Helicopter Rescue Award. George Bain and Alasdair Campbell went to Buckingham Palace to receive Queen's Gallantry Medals. Campbell Bosanquet and Brian Johnstone were awarded the Queen's Commendation for Valuable Services in the Air.

As a result of their success the Board of Trade awarded British Airways a contract to provide a 24-hour-a-day air/sea rescue service in the Shetlands. And on 30 September 1979, work was completed on a lighthouse that now sits on the menacing Ve Skerries – a warning to all shipping.

Elinor Viking's sacrifice had not been in vain.

13

Dave Bullock – The Courage of the Winchman

The American A-10 Thunderbolt is not a sleek aeroplane. Her lumpy lines, H-shaped tailplane and twin turbofans bolted like afterthoughts to the rear of the fuselage, make her a weird-looking craft, a far cry from the streamlined shapes of most modern warplanes. Designated a close-support aircraft she is, in truth, little more than a flying tank, a slow-moving, heavily armoured weapon platform created specifically to wreak havoc on enemy ground forces. For this purpose she is equipped with a remarkable seven-barrelled gun that can burp cannon shells at the astonishing rate of 4,200 a minute.

She has all the grace of a corrugated-iron privy, but her pilots love the tough 53-foot airframe, designed to absorb murderous ground fire and still stay aloft. They love, too, the generous armour-plating that protects them. They revel in her manoeuvrability and awesome firepower. And will not hear a word against her.

A few minutes after 9 a.m. on Tuesday, 18 November 1980, a pair of Thunderbolts from Bentwaters USAF base near Ipswich were flying northwards towards the Wash on a training exercise. They jinked and weaved across the featureless flatlands of East Anglia like a brace of startled, olive-green snipe, dragging in their wake a quiet half-whistle, half-moan, the distinctive cry of the A-10. As ever, they were hunting in twos.

Flying at combat speed of around 400 miles per hour, they twisted along in the peculiar corkscrewing technique evolved for their unique role. A strange aerial ballet, it looks for all the world like two butterflies playing follow-my-leader through a field of summer flowers. The sudden swoops and banks serve a twofold purpose – to throw enemy ground gunners off their aim and to enable each pilot to keep watch over his comrade's tail.

Now they were nearing the Wash, about to overfly the village of Itteringham, 6 miles south of the Norfolk coastal town of Sheringham. They were still twisting, pulling towards each other, then turning to veer apart, as they followed their complicated flight pattern through the wintry skies.

But this time they got it wrong.

For all their sedate combat speed, they closed with brutal suddenness. In desperation the pilots twisted their controls hard over in the opposite direction, each man reefing back hard to find an escape route from the fast-narrowing gap. A split-second more and they might have got away with no more than a moment's fright, a flutter of the heart and a story to tell that night with rueful smiles over a beer in the officers' club. But though both machines were now standing on end, their 57 foot wingspans vertical and their engines howling, they were tragically, a hair's breadth too close.

A shuddering jar shook the aircraft as they slammed together like two billiard balls colliding. They hit belly to belly and cannoned off in opposite directions. Metal debris fluttered behind them as feathers fly from a pair of fighting cocks. From the cockpit of one appeared a brief sunburst flare as the pilot yanked the firing handle of his ejector seat. He was flung clear, a dark, tumbling blob against the November sky. As stunned villagers watched the shape resolve itself into a man above whom a parachute blossomed to life, the aircraft tumbled into the ground and erupted in a ball of fire.

The second Thunderbolt was still airborne – hurt, but capable of flight. With the instinct of a wounded gamebird, it turned for home, wheeling out over the North Sea in a long, shaky curve, before heading south for Bentwaters. At the controls was Lieutenant Colonel William Olsen. Though qualified to fly the Thunderbolt, he was currently serving a ground tour as an operations officer. That day's sortie had included him so that he could keep his hand in with a couple of hours of flying a plane instead of a desk. Once clear of the land, he began travelling parallel with the coastline over angry waves whipped by a Force Eight gale.

Rudder, elevators and ailerons – he gingerly tested his controls. All seemed to be working properly. The engines sounded healthy enough; none of the instruments was showing a warning or behaving abnormally. Incredibly, it seemed he had escaped unscathed from what, in most cases, would have been a fatal mid-air collision. But as the battered Thunderbolt howled down the East Anglian coast, he prepared for one final test – to see if he could lower the undercarriage.

If not, if the doors to the wheel bays had been buckled and rendered useless by the impact, jamming so the wheels couldn't be lowered, then there was no point in continuing back to Bentwaters. A normal landing would be out of the question while a wheels-up one could damage the aircraft – and probably himself – beyond repair. Better by far in that case, to head back over the land then turn to point the nose out to sea again and 'bang out' with the ejector seat. The A-10 would then fly out to sea and crash in her own time.

The colonel selected 'wheels down', his eyes anxiously scanning the instrument panel for the three green lights that would tell him his gear was down and safely locked. Behind and below, deep in her innards, the aircraft flexed her powerful hydraulic muscles and groaning like a woman contracting in labour, pushed downwards against the resistance of her damaged underbelly. Hesitantly, the buckled doors slanted open to make way for the unfolding undercarriage legs. But as the gear angled down it somehow opened a hidden wound in a damaged hydraulic line.

The wound became a gaping split. Dark fluid gushed forth like blood pouring from a severed vein and from that moment the aircraft began to die. In the cockpit Olsen felt his flying controls, all hydraulic-powered, stiffen beneath his

177

hands and feet as the vital fluid bled from the system. Within seconds rigor mortis had set in. The controls were immovably locked. Even using all his strength, he could not budge them. The dying plane began to lose height.

Calmly he tightened the straps attaching him to the ejector seat and radioed a final 'Mayday' to enable listeners on the ground to get a fix on his position. He would have to take his chances in the sea now, for there was no possibility of reaching land, but with luck a rescue helicopter would be on the way already and would winch him to safety within minutes.

Colonel Olsen reached for the firing handle of his ejector seat . . .

*   *   *

It was 9.28 a.m. The crewroom of 'C' Flight, 202 Squadron on the edge of the airfield at RAF Coltishall, was crowded as duty helicopter crews prepared for a shift change. Bellingall's crew was due to hand over to the newcomers in two minutes. Servicemen, however, are not clock-watchers and change-overs usually developed into a few minutes of chat over coffee and cigarettes.

'Want some coffee, Jim?' Dave Bullock, the winchman, asked Bellingall. Though the latter was a flight lieutenant and Bullock a master air loadmaster (aircrew warrant officer), such easy familiarity is normal in the close-knit world of search-and-rescue helicopters. Before Bellingall could answer, the 'squawk box' echoed tinnily through the smoke-filled room. This was the intercom link between air traffic control and 'C' Flight's modest operations room.

It was hard to decipher the message for several people were talking at once and, John Reeson, the burly winch operator, frowned with concentration as he sought to unravel what was being said. Satisfied finally that he had understood, he gave a brief acknowledgement and clicked the switch into the 'off' position.

'Mid-air collision,' he announced to the others. 'Two Yanks have hit each other near Itteringham. One's exploded

– the other may still be flying.' Coffee and shift change forgotten, the two crews busied themselves; Jim Bellingall and his men for immediate take-off; the fresh crew going on to immediate readiness in case they, too, were scrambled.

Minutes later six men streamed out of the door of the crewroom and, bending into a 45 mile-an-hour wind that buffeted off the sea, ran for the waiting yellow Sea King helicopter. Into the captain's seat went Bellingall. His second pilot, 28-year-old Flight Lieutenant Adrian Nockles, took the other. Behind them, in a curtained section containing radar and radios, was Reeson, a master air electronics officer and the winch operator. Further aft Dave Bullock helped to make their two passengers – a medical officer and fireman in a flameproof suit – as comfortable as possible.

The Sea King's twin engines shrieked to a crescendo and the ungainly machine lifted upwards from the old Battle of Britain airfield towards the fast-scudding clouds overhead. At an airspeed of 130 miles per hour it clattered across the flat Norfolk landscape towards the distant plume of oily black smoke, quickly shredded by the gale, that marked the grave of the Thunderbolt that had crashed at Itteringham.

But that was not their objective. With little more than two minutes to fly before reaching the hamlet, fresh instructions came over the radio: Bellingall and his crew must turn east and search for the second pilot who had now ditched over the sea. In the meantime, the standby Sea King had been scrambled to pick up the pilot who had baled out over land.

*   *   *

Olsen choked and gagged as a breaking wave forced salt water into his mouth. He came up gasping for air but the sea's terrible cold seemed to squeeze every breath out of his body. He was stunned and disoriented after the traumatic mule-kick of ejection and the shock of hitting the water.

179

Worse, by a wretched irony the parachute which had saved his life was now threatening to kill him – surely a bitter twist of fate. Unable to free himself of its harness, and with its canopy inflated by the gale, he was being dragged along headfirst through the 15-foot waves at terrifying speed. His helmet, along with his one-man dinghy, had been snatched away during the blast of ejection. Seas broke constantly over his face as he planed through the water like a child's puppet trailing on the end of its strings. Sometimes the parachute canopy deflated and his madcap progress eased, but then another gust of wind would take it, jerking him into motion again.

Unlike the RAF flyer whose parachute harness clicks into a quick-release box over his midriff, Americans have parachutes with fasteners attached to each shoulder harness. Each buckle must be squeezed between thumb and forefinger to free the wearer from his 'chute, a straightforward enough procedure under normal circumstances. But subject the buckles to strain and it is like trying to unravel a knot in a taut rope. The more tension on the fastenings, the stronger your fingers and thumbs must be to operate the release mechanism.

That was Olsen's problem. The Force Eight gale that was dragging his parachute eastwards was exerting a fearful pressure on the fasteners. Despite squeezing with all his strength they wouldn't move. He was weakening fast, retching and fighting for every breath as the runaway parachute trawled him through the water, jerking him, not over the wave crests, but through them. Dimly, through stinging, water-filled eyes, he was aware of a shape hanging in the sky above him and, as though from afar, he heard the rhythmic clamour of a helicopter. Though consciousness was fast receding, he managed a feeble wave of his arm. But no one came, no winchman twisting down towards him on the end of the wire to pluck him from the sea. Just the helicopter sitting above, battering the waves with its downwash. He waved again: *Why didn't some sonofabitch come to help?*

Then there was only blackness and silence.

The British Airways Wessex, for that was what it was, could not help Olsen. For it was not equipped with a winch. Flying in the vicinity, it had responded to the American's 'Mayday', but its civilian crew were powerless to do any more than keep vigil over the downed pilot and wait for the RAF to arrive . . .

As Bellingall's Sea King approached, the Wessex wheeled thankfully out of the way to give him a clear run over the lonely figure floating on his back in the outflung pose of a crucified man. At first the RAF men tried to hover over Olsen – only to see him disappear from sight as his gale-filled parachute dragged him backwards through the water. They followed while John Reeson, like a bus conductor clinging to the platform rail to help his driver reverse, hung out of the starboard door giving instructions to the pilots: *Back 10 . . . back 10 . . . back 10 . . . right a bit . . . a bit more . . . back 10 . . .*

Blindly, the men at the controls flew backwards at a height of 40 feet keeping station above the American pilot. To their astonishment their rough calculations showed that he was being pulled through the water at between 12 and 14 knots!

If he wasn't dead already he soon would be unless they managed to fish him to safety very quickly. And that meant that Dave Bullock had to go down for him. Experienced though he was, the 38-year-old Caithness man knew it would be no picnic; that he, too, would take an awful battering in those violent, icy seas. Normally the joker of the crew, he was for once strangely quiet as he volunteered to be lowered into the water.

As he went over the side, John Reeson, operating the winch control beside the cargo door, watched his progress: 'The seas were rough, but Dave managed to get straight to the man and hang on to him. The parachute was dragging them both through the water at a hell of a pace and I was having to give constant instructions to the pilots so we could stay above them. I saw Dave clip his harness to the American's harness and attempt to cut through the parachute lines with his knife. Trouble was half the canopy was in the water;

those lines were slack, just floating about under the surface. The part of the canopy that was clear of the water remained inflated, keeping the topmost lines taut.

'He kept trying to get his knife on the slack ones. Once he'd cut through those, the taut ones would be no problem – one cut and they'd part, then I'd be able to winch them both up. But in the middle of all the waves and spray he couldn't see the underwater ones. He kept trying to grab them, but they were just waving about like seaweed, out of sight under the surface.

'He gave a hand signal, telling me to winch him just clear of the water, and I knew he wanted lifting a few feet so he could get a better view.'

Reeson talked the pilots down to about 15 feet above the sea, then nudged the winch switch into the 'Up' position. The two fliers, Scot and American, came out of the water. So, too, did the accursed parachute canopy, filling instantly with wind and billowing up towards the Sea King's tail rotor. Had it become enmeshed with the spinning blades it would have dragged the helicopter out of the sky.

'You could almost hear the cable humming it was so taut,' Reeson said afterwards. 'As fast as I could, I unwound the cable to dump them back in the sea and take the weight off the wire.'

But the strain had proved too much. One by one the twisted steel fibres began to part and, with a suddenness that rocked the Sea King, the cable broke, pitching the two men back into the water.

'The bloody cable's gone!' Reeson's anguished voice roared over the intercom.

He saw Bullock inflate his lifejacket with its carbon dioxide cylinder and then he and the American were momentarily dragged out of sight as a fresh gust of wind filled the parachute like a spinnaker, tacking them off at a tangent. Swearing, the distraught winch operator reeled in the broken wire and spliced a lead weight to its ragged end. His intention was to lower the weight on to the parachute canopy to deflate it. But when he tried, it just bounced off the balloon-like surface. With all their skill the pilots steered backwards, trying to keep station above their crewmate and the American to whom he had clipped himself but needing to keep the machine's nose head-on to the 45 mile per hour wind. Despite his own appalling predicament, Bullock continued to try to keep the colonel's head out of the water, fighting for the other man's life as vigorously as he was fighting for his own.

Reeson freed one of the Sea King's emergency dinghies and chucked it over the side. It landed close to the two men. But, driven by the howling wind, it tore past them at the pace of a speedboat. 'Even if Dave had managed to catch hold it was travelling so fast it would have pulled his arm out of its socket,' Reeson recalled.

The intercom was busy as the three remaining crewmen discussed – and rejected – a number of desperate measures to try to save their friend. *Shove another dinghy over the side*? They already had proof that the wind could carry it away. *Land on the sea?* Though a Sea King is capable of floating, it would quickly capsize in such heavy seas, almost certainly killing all five men aboard. *Reeson to go over the side and try to swim to the two?* What then? With no means of winching him back aboard, that option would be almost certain suicide. If there had been a chance, even a slim one, he would have gone willingly but there wasn't a hope in hell. His death would be pointless.

Gradually the intercom fell silent. There was nothing left to say. Within seconds of the winch cable snapping they had radioed for help; all they could do now was wait for it to arrive. With a feeling of helplessness and profound sadness John Reeson watched his friend's weakening struggles as he and the American were pulled through the whitecaps, often obliterated from sight by breaking water.

He had been Bullock's instructor when the latter had gone through the Search and Rescue Training Unit at RAF Valley in Anglesey. Many a night they had swapped pints of beer and jokes in the Sergeants' Mess. Bullock had always been the live-wire who could raise a smile even at the tensest moments – yet he was good at his job, a hard and willing worker.

Now all Reeson could do was stand and watch him die. Close to tears, he watched the winchman's struggles grow feebler until they stopped altogether. He and the American began rolling over in the water like those metal spinners used by anglers to lure fish. Then Reeson knew they were both dead.

The bodies were recovered by paramedics aboard a USAF CH53 'Jolly Green Giant' helicopter – Bullock first, then Olsen. By then they had been dragged a further 5 miles by the parachute. As the Sea King escorted the big American machine towards an emergency landing ground near Norwich hospital, her crew received the confirmation they were dreading.

'Both are Delta' came an American voice over the radio.

The RAF men were in no mood for codes. 'What?' asked Adrian Nockles, the second pilot. 'Say again.'

'Dead. Both dead.' was the reply.

After they'd written out the inevitable reports back at Coltishall, after an officer had been despatched to break the terrible news to Bullock's wife Pat, at her home in Aylsham, Bellingall, and his crew were sent off duty, Adrian Nockles, the youngest member, arrived home, still unable to accept that a man he had been talking to an hour before was dead. His wife, Anna, was suffering from 'flu. 'Come on,' he told her grimly. 'We're going to the pub.' Puzzled, she didn't argue but slipped on her coat and followed him out of the house. Only when he had downed a large Scotch, then chased it with two or three more, did he tell the story of that terrible morning.

'When I'd drunk far too much for my own good I went home and keeled over in bed,' he recalled. 'I'm not the sort of person who breaks down with grief; getting drunk was my way of clearing it from my mind.'

The following August, Master Air Loadmaster David Edward Bullock, the first RAF winchman to be killed during a rescue, was posthumously awarded the George Medal for gallantry.

The citation said:

Despite the unique and considerable difficulties created by the inflated parachute he calmly went about the business of attempting to recover the pilot to the helicopter as quickly and as safely as possible.

He was close to success when the cable broke. Well aware of the very dangerous situation created by this catastrophic turn of events, he had every opportunity over a period of three or four minutes to disconnect himself from the pilot and save his own life. However, consciously, and with conspicuous courage, he chose to remain with the pilot in the hope of saving him.

For a search and rescue man there could be no finer epitaph.

14

Chris Folland – Visibility Nil

The ratings' married quarters at Royal Naval Air Station Culdrose near Helston, Cornwall, looked picturesque for once as a silent blanket of snow settled in the bright glow of the street lamps. The night was bitterly cold, and a strong, ragged wind whined in from the east.

Chris Folland was drifting in that delicious hazy limbo between wakefulness and sleep when the peace was shattered by the high-pitched beep of the radio-pager that stood alongside his loose change on the bedside table. He said a short word not normally used in polite company and slid from the warm depths of the bed into which he had climbed only a few minutes earlier. His watch, glowing greenly in the darkness, read 11.46. Fran, his attractive, dark-haired wife, grumbled sleepily from her cocoon of blankets.

'Sorry, love, they're buzzing me,' he told her as he scrambled into jeans and sweater. 'I'm off to the phone to see what's up. You stay where you are and go back to sleep.'

Fran Folland had been married to the Fleet Air Arm man long enough to know that the electronic ball and chain he called 'that bloody bleeper' did not summon him for anything other than an emergency. With remarkable speed she found herself wide awake.

'No,' she yawned. 'It's a lousy night out there, so I shan't sleep until you're back. I'll make myself a hot drink and wait up for you.'

Folland, a lanky 27-year-old, blew her a kiss and slipped quietly out of the bedroom. Downstairs, he wrapped his issue raincoat around himself and stepped out and into the icy feathers of snow, shivering at the glacial temperature.

Snow squeaked under his shoes as he slithered over the road to the pool of light cast by the naked bulb of the GPO telephone kiosk. Not or the first time did he curse the fact that as a mere rating – albeit a relatively senior one – he did not qualify for a phone in his married quarter, even though, on occasions like this, vital minutes could be lost.

He dialled 4121 and fed a coin into the slot. 'Leading Aircrewman Folland,' he said. 'Someone was buzzing me.'

Tersely the officer in the Culdrose operations room briefed him. A trawler, the *Ben Asdale*, had struck rocks in nearby Falmouth Bay and was foundering with about a dozen men on board. Culdrose was planning to launch a rescue helicopter. Folland, as standby winchman, was needed for the mission.

'Right sir,' he acknowledged. 'I'll be there in five minutes.'

Sliding awkwardly on the treacherous surface, he ran back across the road and slid behind the wheel of his car. In the kitchen, filling the kettle for the first of many cups of tea, Fran listened to the whirr of the starter motor outside.

She lit a cigarette and prepared for a long vigil . . .

*   *   *

The airfield at Culdrose, like the rest of the West Country, that night – 30 December 1978 – was at the heart of the worst weather Britain had experienced for a quarter of a century. Massive gales roared in from the east, driving blizzards before them. Thirty-foot waves pounded the shores of Cornwall and Devon and ships scurried for shelter or fled into deep water to ride out the storm in open seas. Slowly, inexorably, the West Country froze to a standstill.

In Falmouth Bay, catching the full brunt of the howling storm, the *Ben Asdale's* demise had been fast and brutal.

187

Battered by huge seas, the 350-ton trawler from North Shields had lost her steering. A nearby Soviet factory ship, the 13,087-ton *Antartika* had rushed to her assitance and despite appalling conditions had managed to get a line aboard. Two of her engineers had gallantly volunteered to help and had been transferred to the helpless trawler.

But soon afterwards the line had parted and their shipmates had been forced to watch helplessly as the Force Nine gale drove the British vessel towards rocks at the foot of the cliffs of Maen Porth, a picturesque cove 3 miles south of Falmouth. Minutes later she struck and rolled over on to her port side. Listing at 80 degrees, she began to break up as, time and again, mountainous seas flung her against the unyielding rocks.

Of the 14 men aboard – 12 crew and two Russians – six chose to abandon ship and take their chances in the boiling surf. The shore was, after all, tantalizingly close – only a few yards away.

Three made it, thanks to the heroism of a trio of brothers, Michael, Peter and Graham Billcliffe, local men who scrambled down the rocks and plunged into the sea to drag the exhausted, half-drowned men to safety. Three others, among them one of the Soviet engineers, were beyond reach and perished in the maelstrom.

That left eight men aboard the *Ben Asdale* . . . eight freezing, frightened men for whom time was fast running out. Attempts to rig a breeches buoy had already failed. Falmouth Lifeboat had burrowed her way through mountainous waves, only to find that she could get no closer than 200 yards from the wreck in those shallow, treacherous seas. With hope quickly fading, the storm strengthening by the minute and the seas growing wilder, the coastguards had decided to call for the Navy.

Captain Jock Tofts, RN, the station commander of Culdrose, was in a dilemma. The airfield's duty search and rescue Sea King helicopter had earlier been despatched to Perranporth on a mercy mission. So bad was the weather it had been unable to make it back to base and had been forced to land at Marazion. Now he was being asked to launch another helicopter in conditions in which no sane man would normally fly.

Visibility was less than 500 yards in constant snow, the cloud base was 200 feet, the temperature was hovering around zero and winds were gusting up to 50 miles per hour. The forecast prophesied that the weather would get worse in the very near future. What should Tofts do? Should he wait to see if the coastguards or the lifeboat could somehow find a way of taking the eight trawlermen to safety? Or should he expose a helicopter and its crew to danger, even death? The doubts he faced were a very real example of the old adage about the loneliness of command. The decision, right or wrong, had to be entirely his own.

In the operations room he looked round at the standby crew who had been called in. There was the first pilot, Lieutenant Tony Hogg, 29; the aircraft's captain and observer 36-year-old Lieutenant Commander Mike Norman; second pilot, Lieutenant Larry Jeram-Croft; and winchman Folland. With them was a volunteer, Leading Medical Assistant Brian Steele. Though not aircrew, he had offered to fly the mission in case survivors needed medical attention.

Soon came the news that the coastguards and lifeboat had failed. By then Captain Tofts had already reached his decision. 'We'll launch a chopper,' he ordered.

At 1.45 a.m. helicopter No. 592 took off in heavy snow. Although a 706 Squadron machine, her standby crew was from 814 Squadron. Swaying and bouncing in the gusts of wind she clattered off into the filthy night – not due east to where the *Ben Asdale* was dying, but south-west and out to sea across the Loe Bar.

To the east of Culdrose lies high ground which would force them upwards, close to the clouds and the freezing level of 500 feet where, within minutes, the big blue helicopter would become cloaked in heavy layers of ice that would begin blocking engine intakes, slowly choking her twin jet engines. So the detour via Loe Bar was unavoidable. On this route, 592 could stay below the danger height by hugging the coastline only 200 feet above the waves.

189

Norman, as captain and observer, had the responsibility of navigating the 9-ton Sea King to Maen Porth. Crouched over his glowing radar screen in the 25-foot-long main cabin he relayed constant course changes to the two pilots on the flight deck – no easy matter when huge seas were constantly cluttering the picture on the screen.

Twenty minutes after take-off, Norman guided the cumbersome machine over Maen Porth. But the Navy fliers looked in vain for any signs of the wreck. The snow was worsening by the minute and they could barely make out the little cove or even South Cornwall coastline.

Then, out of the darkness, came a voice over the radio, faint and distorted by interference. It came from the coastguards' Land Rover parked on the clifftop.

'OK, I see you,' it said. 'Keep coming as you are.'

But it wasn't as simple as that. To hover in any wind over 20 knots, a Sea King must have her nose into wind, yet the storm by now was raging at Force 10. The best way to have approached the *Ben Asdale* would have been to come in from the open sea, thus avoiding the unseen cliffs and the additional turbulence they would cause, but to attempt to hover tail-on to winds gusting to 60 miles per hour and more would have been a short cut to disaster.

'We'll have to approach over the land,' Mike Norman told the pilots over the intercom. 'It's the only way we can stay head-on to the wind.'

Tony Hogg, the first pilot, gained height as he groped like a blind man to steer his machine over land. When the altimeter showed 400 feet he swept forward, knowing he could not maintain that height for long without the Sea King beginning to ice up.

Behind him Mike Norman was radioing the coastguards. 'I will overfly you,' he said. 'Get your searchlight shining vertically to show us where you are. When we see you we will make a rapid descent beyond the cliffs over open sea.'

The coastguards had barely acknowledged the message and switched on their searchlight when a terrific roar blotted out even the tumult of the storm. Landing lights and red beacons blazing, the Sea King burst through the blizzard above their heads. The bedraggled men ducked instinctively in their Land Rover.

Over their radio came a triumphant cry from Mike Norman: 'Visual!' He had spotted their powerful beam. That behind him, he knew he could safely order the pilots to descend, secure in the knowledge that they were clear of land.

Abruptly the engine note changed as the Sea King dipped down towards the white, confused waters of the cove. In the brief seconds of the bouncing, frightening descent into the unknown, the helicopter men caught one fleeting glimpse of the *Ben Asdale*. The radio altimeter showed their height of 50 feet but by the time the pilots had managed a steady hover, they were already 1,000 or so yards out to sea. They had overshot and there was only one way to get back to the wreck. They would have to fly backwards.

In normal circumstances a helicopter is perfectly capable of reversing, but there was nothing normal about that wild New Year's Eve. Gusts of wind were tossing the Sea King about like a discarded balloon, no one on board could see much other than the whirling kaleidoscope of snowflakes and the occasional seething whitecaps of angry waves; all too easily they could back too far and hit the cliffs, or entangle themselves in the *Ben Asdale*'s gyrating masts and rigging.

Yet, if the trawlermen were to be saved, it was the only way.

Mike Norman called up the coastguards: 'Can you see us?'

'Yes, we can just see your lights.'

'Can you con us back into cove?'

For a long moment there was silence, broken at last by the voice of the coastguard crackling over the ether: 'Message understood. We will con you backwards into the cove.'

Norman shoved himself out of his seat by the radar set and crouched in the open doorway on the starboard side of the fuselage, flinching at the icy blast that cut into him with scalpel sharpness. The next bit was going to be somewhat tricky.

Situated on a Sea King's cabin wall a few inches inside and forward of the cabin door, is a control called the auxiliary hover trim, a tiny joystick which allows the observer some limited control of the machine.

Normally it is used for small critical movements during hovering when the observer, with good downward vision denied to the pilots who sit some 15 feet in front of him, is best placed to position the aircraft above a target. Mike Norman's idea was simple: the pilots would use their controls to maintain height at 50 feet above the churning waves while he, leaning out of the door and squinting into the blackness, would use the auxiliary lever trim to jockey them astern towards the *Ben Asdale*.

Slowly the extraordinary backwards flight inched them into the blind cove as the Lieutenant Commander juggled with the auxiliary hover trim to try to obey the coastguard's unending chant of directions. 'Left – left – left. Steady . . . keep 'er coming at that. Right a shade . . . right . . . steady . . . left a bit . . . left . . . hold it on that heading . . .'

Melting snow and freezing salt spray ran down his face but Mike Norman was past feeling the cold, past everything but concentrating on the daunting, demanding task he had set himself.

'How long it took I just don't know,' he recalled later. 'It seemed to take an age, but then finally we could see the *Ben Asdale*, lying on her side about 70 feet from the foot of the cliffs.

'She was in a terrible state, rolling wildly on the rocks with huge seas carrying right across her. By now the coastguards had got a searchlight shining on her and we could clearly see the survivors clinging to her. One, who later turned out to be the other Russian engineer, the mate of the dead one, was in the hawsehole near the bows, almost constantly under water. The others were hanging on near the bridge. We decided to go for the man in the bows first because he looked in a bad way.'

Beside Norman in the doorway was Chris Folland, the winchman. All through the dramatic backwards flight he, too, had been leaning out into the night, helping the Captain steer the uncertain course into the unknown. Now, pale and apprehensive, he was ready for the next stage of the

(Express Newspapers)

The wreck of the Dan-Air HS 748 is hauled from the sea at the end of the runway of Sumburgh Airport, Shetland

Liz Cowe, the Dan-Air hostess who became the heroine of the Sumburgh air disaster

(Express Newspapers)

(Ministry of Defence)

Winching from the deck of a warship

An RAF winchman lifts a survivor to a search and rescue Sea King helicopter

(Express Newspapers)

Captain Stanley Key of British European Airways. He piloted
the ill-fated Trident which crashed soon after take-off from
London Heathrow. He and 117 others died – then disquieting
stories of a quarrel and a vendetta began to emerge

operation. Trussed in a rubber immersion suit, his harness clipped to the winch hook, he prepared to be lowered into the turmoil raging below.

'I was too preoccupied to be actually scared,' he told me. 'But I wasn't looking forward to trying to get aboard the trawler. She was bouncing and rolling like a pig. To put myself on to her without injuring myself or getting tangled up was going to take a hell of a lot of doing.'

The young Devonian stretched his 6 foot 4½ inch frame and touched the observer on the shoulder. 'OK, sir, I'm ready,' he said.

Norman looked up at the leading aircrewman towering above him, then peered out of the doorway at the raging seas and the shifting, groaning shipwreck. He shook his head.

'Unhook yourself, Folland,' he ordered. 'There's no way I'm going to put you down into that lot. They'll have to come up by single lift.'

The usual technique for search and rescue missions is to use a double-lift – the winchman going down on the end of the wire to loop a canvas strop over a survivor and accompanying him on the ascent back to the helicopter. Single-lift technique involves lowering an empty strop and leaving the survivors to work out for themselves what to do next.

Obediently Folland unhooked himself and the double-lift strop from the winch hook, deftly substituting a single-lift strop from the bundle of spare stretchers, ropes and blankets he had prudently loaded before take-off. Crouching back beside his captain in the doorway, he had his hand on the winch control, a few inches above the auxiliary hover trim. He clicked it down and began lowering the strop towards the Russian in the hawsehole as Mike Norman rocked the little joystick back and forth to try and maintain position above the target.

Circling and spinning in the wind and the rotor's downdraught, the canvas strop swung through driving spray towards the sodden seaman. Judging the moment nicely, Folland managed to drop the strop into his hands. Stiffly, with clumsy, uncoordinated movements, the freezing Russian managed to get the loop round himself. Folland knocked the winch switch up and watched with satisfaction as the man was yanked up into space.

Dragging him in through the doorway and getting him out of the strop was hard work, for the survivor was virtually unconscious. He was suffering badly from hypothermia; only a few minutes more in those icy seas would have killed him. Brian Steele, the volunteer medic, took over, wrapping the engineer in blankets and trying to chafe some warmth back into his trembling limbs.

Meanwhile, Folland was lowering the winch strop once more, this time towards the huddle of survivors clinging to the guard rails near the bridge. He waited patiently while the exhausted seamen struggled to get one of their number into the strop. Someone gave him a shaky thumbs-up sign and he hit the winch switch once more. He helped Norman drag the second survivor aboard. He was blue with cold, shivering uncontrollably but he managed to gasp 'Thank you' as they shoved him into Steele's arms.

Two gone; six to go.

It was at this point that the Sea King crew found themselves with a new problem. Even with only two survivors aboard, the after part of the main cabin was already crowded and Folland and Norman were having trouble working in the confined space. Yet they could not move the survivors into the forward section because, as long as Norman continued to operate the auxiliary hover trim, his body blocked the narrow gangway that led forward past the radios, radar and anti-submarine electronics.

As the strop went down for the third time, he was obliged to hand full control back to the two pilots and help Steele manhandle the two trawlermen forward. By now, observer and winchman were so drenched from leaning out of the doorway that water had seeped into the wiring of their helmets and was having an adverse effect on communications. Speech over the intercom began breaking up into little more than a series of frustrating crackles and high-pitched whines. Soon it became impossible to hear anything at all and information had to be relayed by a combination of hoarse shouting and exaggerated pantomime.

Literally flying blind, the two pilots struggled as best they could to hover steadily, but just as the winch strop was grabbed by the third survivor a monumental gust of wind flung the Sea King violently to port.

With cruel force the trawlerman was yanked off his insecure perch and swung in a mad arc beneath the aircraft. The engines blared as the pilots fought to regain control. Chris Folland paid out cable at 200 feet per minute – four times the normal rate – in an effort to dampen down the crazy swing of the man on the end of the wire.

The 62-foot, five-bladed main rotor scythed in over the cliff tops 'almost clipping the grass', said one bystander later. Hogg and Jeram-Croft hauled the Sea King back from almost certain disaster with little more than inches to spare, but despite Folland's quick thinking in paying out more cable, the trawlerman in the strop was having a wild perilous ride.

As the helicopter righted herself, he swung upwards in a monumental curve, almost to the same altitude as the rescue machine. With a solid 'thunk' the toughened steel cable hit the fuselage, biting into the glass-fibre fairing aft of the cabin door and cutting a deep furrow there.

Already Folland was reeling in the survivor. He rose to within a few feet of the door, but then the trapped cable jammed solid in glass-fibre made tacky by the friction. The winchman swore. What a lousy stroke of luck. He dare not carry on winching – already there were signs that some of the cable's steel fibres were stripping; the added strain might easily burn out the winch motor. Yelling at the top of his voice he explained the situation to Mike Norman.

The captain's brain raced as he tried to work out what to do. Head inland and touch down in a field? Too risky – the pilots were flying totally blind; without runway lights they could easily crash in the blizzard. Turn back to Culdrose with the man dangling on the wire? No chance – he would have frozen to death before they were even halfway there.

As he ponderd on which would be the lesser evil, Folland, held only by his safety harness, was hanging head down out of the doorway, struggling with every ounce of strength to free the wire from the deep channel it had cut into the fairing.

He was gasping for breath when he finally flopped back into the cabin. 'No good, sir,' he shouted. 'There's not a cat in hell's chance, not with his weight holding the wire taut like that.'

'Can you lower him?' Norman yelled.

The winchman clicked the switch and the man jerked downwards a few feet.

'Good,' nodded the observer. 'I've got an idea.'

It was not one he relished. It could easily kill the man they were trying to save, but it was the only way he could think of. He stumbled forward to the flight deck to explain to the pilots what they must do . . .

The man on the end of the wire, 46-year-old Nigel Robinson, was all-in, drifting close to unconsciousness. Vaguely he wondered what the hell the hold-up was; why they hadn't lifted him inside. Then he felt the helicopter surge forward towards the open sea. To his horror he felt the cable unwinding, lowering him towards racing mountains of white water. His cry of horror choked off as he hit the sea . . .

The moment Robinson's weight came off the cable Folland was hanging out of the doorway, wrestling with the steel cord. It freed with a jerk. 'Take her up!' he bawled. As the Sea King reared upwards, the winchman was scrambling to his feet, jamming the switch upwards for the fast wind-in.

Sixty seconds later he dragged Robinson, choking and blue with cold, across the threshold of the door and handed him over to Brian Steele. Once more Mike Norman resumed his position in the doorway to guide the pilots backwards into position over the *Ben Asdale*.

Without the intercom, and with snow falling thicker than ever, it was virtually impossible. The officer cursed the black, foul night and seriously considered abandoning the rescue and flying back to Culdrose while the three survivors they had already rescued were still alive. But then his spirit rebelled; he could not just leave the remaining five to their fate. He yelled to the pilots: 'Keep coming back! Left . . . left . . . keep coming.' Somehow, God knows how, he found the dying trawler again and Folland put the winch wire down once more.

Everyone's memories of the latter stages of the rescue are vague . . . an endless nightmare of noise, peril and frustration, of yelling voices growing hoarser by the minute, of body-aching tiredness, confusion and fear. Yet, at 3.30 a.m. – 105 long minutes after take-off – the eighth survivor was finally brought aboard. By then Mike Norman had long been reduced to passing hastily scribbled notes to the pilots. As the exhausted trawlerman swung in through the door, he wrote the final one:

'Head east for two miles, then south,' – first leg of the journey home.

The trip was like a bad dream. As Folland and Steele worked to keep the eight survivors alive, Mike Norman had to navigate back to base. His radar and radios were shaky, the airfield's ground-control approach radar was out of commission because of a power failure and the pilots could see nothing but whirling snowflakes. Yet somehow they managed to put Sea King 592 right in the middle of the helipad. It was a remarkable ending to a truly remarkable rescue.

Months later the *London Gazette* described the mission as 'one of the most dangerous rescues undertaken by a Naval aircraft in recent years'.

That was part of the citation that conferred the Air Force Cross on Mike Norman and Tony Hogg; the Queen's Commendation for Valuable Service in the Air to Larry Jeram-Croft and Chris Folland; and the Queen's Commendation for Brave Conduct to Brian Steele.

*　　*　　*

Folland slid wearily behind the wheel of his car and turned the ignition key. With the rest of the crew, he had just spent two hours manhandling 592 through a howling blizzard into the hangar while the big wheels of the towing tractor had spun uselessly on sheet ice as smooth as glass.

The engine coughed into life. Selecting first gear, he nosed cautiously out of his parking spot and turned towards married quarters. He had gone no more than a few yards when massive snow drifts brought him to a slithering halt. The engine faltered, coughed and died. It would not restart. Numb with weariness, he climbed from behind the wheel and began trudging through the deep snow, head bowed into the whirling flakes.

It was two long arctic miles to his home. Long before he reached the front drive he could see the yellow pool of light spilling out of the lounge window into the grey snow-streaked dawn.

There, he knew, Fran would be waiting. Breakfast would be rustled up within a few minutes. Bacon and eggs, he fancied, with tomatoes and fried bread. And tea – lots of tea.

He quickened his step.

15

The Mystery of Flight 706

It was at precisely 10.34 on the morning of Saturday, 2 October 1971, that Captain Ed Probert of British European Airways hauled back on the control yoke of Vickers Vanguard G-APEC and felt his wheels part company with Runway 28L at London's Heathrow Airport. Spinning in fine pitch, the propellers of the four Rolls-Royce Tyne turboprops clawed more than 50 tons of aircraft into the grey morning sky. The 40-year-old pilot, with 9,260 flying hours to his credit, raised the undercarriage, trimmed 'Echo-Charlie' to climb and put her in a gentle bank until she was heading eastwards.

Flight BE 706, the morning scheduled service to the Austrian city of Salzburg, 652 miles away, was following a familiar routine. After a few minutes the 'No Smoking' and seatbelt signs clicked off and the 55 passengers unbuckled themselves while the four cabin staff bustled forward to the galley to begin the shuttle of coffee and drinks. For them it would be an easy flight. The big prop-jet could carry up to 139 passengers. With little more than a third that number aboard, they could afford a more leisurely pace on the 2½-hour flight, even during the normally hectic scramble for duty-free goods. At almost 5 miles a minute 'Echo Charlie' whined over the English Channel, bathed in bright sunlight above the clouds, heading for the Belgian coast.

Twenty-seven minutes after take-off, she passed out of the Dover control zone into that of Brussels Air Control

Centre. There it was a routine – if busy – Saturday morning. Air traffic controllers sat at their glowing radar screens, in constant contact with the stream of aircraft en route through their airspace along Green One, a major east-west corridor across Northern Europe.

At 11.01 London time, a duty air traffic controller in the centre, listening on 131.1 megahertz, picked up his first message from 'Echo-Charlie' as she left Dover's airspace. It was probably spoken by John Davies, Ed Probert's 38-year-old first officer:

Good morning, Brussels. Bealine 706 is passing one-eight for one-nine-zero . . . (climbing through 18,000 feet to her normal cruising height of 19,000).

Speaking in English – the lingua franca of the air – the Belgian radioed a brief acknowledgement, confirming that the Vanguard was cleared to continue at that altitude towards Salzburg on Green One. Three minutes later he again heard from 'Echo-Charlie', a routine updating of her position – by now 15 miles closer, near the town of Wulpen. By 11.09, levelling off 3½ miles high, she was approaching the village of Aarsele, 13 miles west of Ghent. Forty-six seconds later – during which time she had covered almost another 4 miles – she transmitted again. The words that filled the headphones caused the Belgian to rear upright with shock.

We're going down – seven-zero-six – we're going down! Mayday! Mayday! Mayday! The international distress code was shouted out by two voices, probably those of First Officer Davies and Captain Probert. Worse was to come as the white-faced controller listened to the brief torrent of horror echoing over the airways. Above the fear-strained voices of the crew he could hear a continuous, mounting whine and strange crunching and blowing noises.

Then: *Mayday! Mayday! Mayday! We're going down vertically! Bealine seven-zero-six out of control . . . out of control! No rudder . . . Aah, this is it!* . . .

At 11.10 and 40 seconds, the transmission cut abruptly.

Routine had turned into nightmare.

From that first strangled *We're going down*! to the instant of impact that brought oblivion to 55 passengers and eight crew, took just 54 seconds. At almost 700 miles an hour, canted 20 degrees beyond the vertical and spinning slowly clockwise, 'Echo-Charlie' hit the ground nose first and disintegrated in a giant kerosene fireball, blasting a 20-foot-deep crater in the soft clay of Flanders. Chunks of metal boomeranged across the flat grassy field near Aarsele, scything through trees and fencing. One spinning piece struck a passing car, slightly injuring one of the petrified occupants.

The Brussels controller sat numbly at his console, repeating with frantic urgency: *Bealine seven-zero-six – do you read me? Hello Bealine seven-zero-six* . . .

The only reply was the mocking hiss of static.

*　　　*　　　*

The Vanguard was a classic case of the right aircraft at the wrong time. Heartened by the runaway success of their Viscount, the world's first turboprop airliner, Vickers tried to consolidate that triumph during the late 1950s with a bigger prop-jet designed to carry twice as many passengers, plus a formidable under-floor freight capacity. But it proved to be an expensive white elephant. By the time the first deliveries – among them 'Echo-Charlie' – went into service with BEA in December 1960, the US swept-wing Boeing 707, a pure-jet uncluttered by propellers, was already dominating the world market, transporting passengers far faster and more economically than the lumbering Vanguard.

Whereas more than 50 operators had bought the Viscount, only one other apart from BEA, Trans-Canada Air Lines, ordered Vanguards. After 43 were built, the production line closed. Vickers wrote off the flop to experience and began concentrating on their own new long-haul jet, the VC-10, itself fated to be something of a failure. For all its commercial shortcomings, however, the Vanguard was a fine aircraft, sturdy and reliable and possessing a magnificent safety record. Why, then, did Flight 706 suddenly fall out of the sky that misty October morning?

For a start, the circumstances were highly unusual. Most air crashes occur during the critical periods of take-off or landing; less than one in 12 happens when an aircraft is at its normal cruising height. This type of accident is also the most difficult to investigate. An out-of-control aircraft falling from high altitude will either break up in mid-air, scattering wreckage over several square miles, or will crash with such force that everything is totally destroyed.

The latter was the fate of 'Echo-Charlie'. As Belgian officials stood beside the still-smouldering carnage at Aarsele, all they could see were tens of thousands of pieces of unrecognizable junk . . . junk, furthermore, which had been subjected to the blowtorch of 25,578 pounds of exploding aviation paraffin. The task of unravelling the mystery seemed hopeless.

Under international law, the nation upon whose soil an air disaster occurs is responsible for the subsequent accident investigation. But Article 26 of the Convention of the International Civil Aviation Organization entitles observers from the aircraft's country of origin to be present and participate in the enquiry.

Within hours of the tragedy, Britain had invoked that right, and three experts from the Accident Investigations Branch (AIB) of the then Department of Trade and Industry were despatched from their base at Farnborough to Heathrow to catch the first flight for Brussels. Their leader was Geoffrey Wilkinson, a 44-year-old aeronautical engineer who had won the Air Force Cross during his 10 years as an RAF officer – later Chief Inspector of the AIB. With him were two engineers, Geoffrey Feltham and his deputy, Jimmy Lett.

Working closely with the Belgians, the start of their quest was simple enough. Within minutes of the crash it was known that a major part of the tailplane had broken off and fallen to earth some 3 kilometres west of where 'Echo-Charlie' had hit the ground and exploded. There could be no doubt that had caused the crash, for an aircraft is held balanced about its centre of gravity by a permanent download on the tail.

Remove that and the nose pitches violently down, just as a seesaw will drop under the weight of a child if his friend hops off the other end.

But why, after 11 years' life and 21,683 flying hours, should the tail suddenly break off? Some clue might well be locked away in the flight data recorder, the 'black box' every civil airliner carries to chart each second of flight. A concentrated search for it began. Next day, in thick mist, it was found in the 600-yard circle of wreckage around the crater. It had been damaged by the terrific impact and its recording wire broken. Despite this, technicians managed to join up the wire so that only one-third of a second of the 35-minute 12-second recording was missing.

Eagerly they replayed it, waiting for it to yield up some evidence to explain the mystery. The tape told them that Flight 706 had been flying normally at 250 knots, at a proper cruising height of 19,000 feet and had been on its correct course of 110 degrees magnetic. Beyond that it told them nothing. For the recording stopped abruptly – just at the point when the Vanguard was flying over a spot 3 kilometres west of Aarsele.

Whatever had caused the tailplane to part company with the rest of the airframe had also stopped the flight recorder, leaving the remaining length of wire enigmatically and frustratingly blank.

By now the story was big news as the human tragedies began to emerge – the fact that Captain Probert should not have made the flight; had been in the captain's seat only to help out a friend who wanted some time off duty . . . that a Yorkshire family of five had perished . . . that one of the dead stewardesses had celebrated her engagement only five days earlier . . .

The headlines brought out the ghouls, too. The roads around Aarsele were jammed with gawpers; an ice-cream van set up business and a peanut vendor from Brussels did a roaring trade. Jackal-like, some people even braved the police cordon to plunder the horribly mutilated corpses of wallets and other valuables. Sickened, the British and Belgian investigators supervised the herculean task of gathering up the countless twisted scraps of the Vanguard to transport them in a fleet of lorries to a hangar at Brussels Airport, well away from the gaze of grisly rubberneckers.

It was not, however, from the main wreckage, but from the remnants of the tailplane, brought from where it had fallen in open country nearly 2 miles away, that the first real clue came. And it was Jimmy Lett, a canny old hand whose long service with the AIB dated back to wartime days of 1944, who first spotted it.

'As soon as we heard the tailplane had been found else-where, the words structural failure shouted at us,' recalled William Tench, Lett's boss and eventual Chief Inspector of the AIB until his retirement in 1981.

'Once it and the other wreckage was spread out on the hanger floor, that was when Jimmy began to put together the jigsaw puzzle. He was examining what was left of one of the tailplanes when we heard him mutter, "Christ almighty, that's a bit odd . . .".'

Lett beckoned Geoffrey Wilkinson – who was to succeed Tench as Chief Inspector – and jabbed at the torn metal with a grubby finger. 'There, those rivets,' he said. 'Take a look. What force is there that could have done that?' Wilkinson stared with fascination at the hunk of wreckage. Most of the rivets were still in place, but the aircraft skin they were supposed to hold was savagely buckled outwards, as though by some internal explosion, until sections of the skin had torn free of the rivet heads.

The Vanguard's tailplanes were of box-spar construction. Two spars, one on the leading edge, the other on the trailing, were rather like the filling of a sandwich – with the skin, top and bottom, acting as the 'bread'. Some incredible force had blasted the sandwich apart. With the 'bread' gone, so too had the structure's rigidity and strength. From that moment there was no power on earth that could have saved the 63 men, women and children on board Flight 706

Could the cause have been a bomb? Perhaps – for a local farmer, Georges Boliaert had told officials, 'We saw what looked like a ball of fire coming down over our fields. The aircraft crashed seconds later.'

The men from Farnborough were sceptical, however. Long experience had taught them that eyewitnesses – 'other than small boys who always tell the truth' avers Bill Tench – possess notoriously inaccurate recall. Though 'Echo-Charlie' had flown to Belfast only days before, it seemed unlikely that the IRA had found a revolutionary form of explosive that left no scorch marks, for there was no trace of burning on the tailplane. That left explosive decompression as the only other feasible explanation.

For the comfort and safety of passengers and crew, most larger civil aircraft have pressurized cabins. As the machine gains height, air is pumped into the cabin to maintain pressure close to that experienced on the ground. To contain that pressure there is an inner airtight seal – similar in principle to the glass container inside a vacuum flask – separating those aboard from the unpressurized sections of the airframe.

At the altitude at which Flight 706 was cruising, the cabin pressure would have been 5.75 pounds per square inch higher than that of the outside atmosphere. If, suddenly, that had managed to escape into an unpressurized section it would cause explosive decompression – pent-up air blasting into the lower pressure area at something approaching the speed of sound. With no means of escaping quickly to the outer atmosphere, the sudden inrush would force itself into every cranny – including, in this instance, the empty space between the two spars inside the 'sandwich' of the tailplane. There, just as a paper bag will explode if you blow into it hard enough, the compressed air had blasted the structure apart, sealing the fate of 'Echo-Charlie' and the 63 people aboard.

Jimmy Lett and his colleagues were now fairly certain they knew *what* had happened, but *why* still eluded them. Explosive decompression is a comparatively rare phenomenon. A door being opened in flight, a window shattering, a projectile puncturing the fuselage, all these things had been known to cause it, but in any of those instances the pressure would have rushed instantly through the hole into the outer atmosphere. For those on board it would have been painful and dangerous, but not necessarily fatal. The fact that cabin pressure had torn with such devasting effect into the tail section led to one inescapable conclusion – somehow the rear pressure dome, the airtight bulkhead dividing the passenger compartment from the tail, must have given way.

For two gruelling and exhausting weeks, often working until the small hours of the morning, the Belgian and British investigators sifted through the torn scraps of metal. Like a prospector who senses gold, Jimmy Lett ploughed in their wake. Twisted engine parts, battered cockpit instruments, fractured hydraulic lines – none of them interested him. He tossed them back on to the 36-ton pile of scrap.

His single-minded search was for as many pieces of the rear pressure dome as he could lay his hands on. Slowly, frustratingly slowly, he began to amass them and, with infinite patience, started to rebuild the dome, fitting together torn shards of alloy in the cold Belgian hangar like someone assembling a complicated jigsaw puzzle.

It was a maddeningly frustrating labour, but at last – half-hidden beneath a mountain of charred rubbish – he found the piece of the concave bulkhead he was seeking. It was battered and unprepossessing, little bigger than a cereal bowl, but his excitement as he examined it could hardly have been greater if it had been a gold ingot.

It was a section from the bottom of the dome, close to where it was joined to the aircraft's deck, just behind the toilet at the after-end of the cabin. Scarring it were ugly stains of corrosion, from which a tear in the metal ran leftwards towards a row of rivets. Excitedly, Lett rooted through the wreckage until he found adjoining pieces which he painstakingly added to his three-dimensional jigsaw.

Gradually, like a photograph coming into being in a developing tank, the picture of what happened swam into focus. Corrosion, probably from tiny spillages of chemicals used in the toilet and from splashes of urine, had slowly eaten into the alloy of the bulkhead, each drop infinitesimally gnawing at the material's strength over the years.

'All materials have an absolute strength,' Bill Tench explained at his retirement home in Cornwall. 'A fatigue failure is the result of a force *less* than that ultimate strength, but with that force being applied and reversed thousands, perhaps millions, of times.'

In other words, the weak spot, flexing and relaxing minutely each time the cabin was pressurized and then depressurized, developed a tiny, fatal crack. Then, just as a beer can that is squeezed flat and bent back and forth will split, the tear grew longer until, 3½ miles above a Belgian village, it tore wide open under the load.

Certain they now had the solution, the AIB men returned to London to put their theory to the test. In Cambridgeshire they decked out the fuselage of a grounded Vanguard with measuring devices and surrounded it with high-speed movie cameras as they recreated the last fatal seconds of 'Echo-Charlie's' existence.

The cabin was pressurized and a small explosive charge was detonated to blow a hole in the rear pressure dome. The effect was instant and dramatic. Compressed air, moving at 580 miles per hour, howled into the tailcone – and the cameras caught, with grim clarity, the sight of the tailplane blowing itself apart.

Eleven months later, the 35-page, highly detailed official report was published. It concluded with one bald sentence:

The accident was caused by the rupture of the rear pressure bulkhead, which led to the separation of both tailplanes in flight and caused the aircraft to dive into the ground.

That was Flight 706's epitaph.

16

Kilo-Foxtrot's Achilles' Heel

Summer was at its height, but there was precious little to show it that bleak Tuesday afternoon at Sumburgh Airport on the southernmost tip of the remote Shetland Islands. A 22-knot wind gusted in from due east, herding before it endless ranks of dirty grey clouds and squalls of slanting rain, whipping the sullen North Sea into 10-foot waves beyond the runway threshold. The temperature was an unseasonal 53 degrees Fahrenheit.

The dreariness of the day – 31 July 1979 – was no match, however, for the high spirits of most of the 44 passengers as they strapped themselves into the seats of 'Kilo-Foxtrot', a Dan-Air HS 748 charter bound for Aberdeen. After toiling on offshore oil rigs in the desolation of Shell's Brent field, they were going on leave, excited by the prospect of seeing wives or girlfriends, thirsty for a booze-up after the enforced abstinence of the drilling platforms. Laughing and joking like schoolchildren on an outing, they readied themselves for take-off as 23-year-old Liz Cowe, trim in her stewardess's uniform, bustled among them. To the winks and wisecracks she smiled politely; she had heard it all before.

They quietened a little for her standard safety briefing but gave a cheer when they saw she was having to use a loudhailer because of a fault on the PA system. Few really listened to what she had to say; they had heard it all before.

On the flight deck, Captain Chris Watson, a 37-year-old from Aberdeenshire, and his 51-year-old copilot, Roy Wells, made their own preparations for departure and taxied to the westernmost end of Runway 09. There they lined up and ran the twin Dart turboprops up to full throttle as the 17-ton aircraft juddered against the leash of her brakes.

No one will ever know which of the two pilots was at the controls when the brakes were released at exactly 5 p.m. and 'Kilo-Foxtrot' began to roll, but if Captain Watson was following Dan-Air regulations it would have been himself – Wells did not have enough flying time on 748s. If the handling pilot *was* Watson, he would have been in the left-hand seat, concentrating on the fast-unwinding concrete strip beyond the rain-spattered windshield, keeping his eyes on the centre-line of the 1,000-yard runway and the white horses breaking on the rocky beach at the end.

Wells would have been holding the two throttle levers wide open and constantly scanning the instruments and array of warning lights to make sure all was well. At 106 miles per hour he would have called 'V1' into his headset microphone – indicating to the captain that they were at the last point at which take-off could be safely abandoned.

By then, 21 seconds after brakes-off, they had travelled 540 yards. Two seconds later – during which another 105 yards had been covered – he would call 'Rotate', meaning the aircraft had reached her take-off speed of 114 miles per hour and that Watson could haul back on the control column and climb away.

That moment came at 23 seconds past 5 p.m. – a moment at which the fate of the two pilots and 15 others aboard 'Kilo-Foxtrot' was sealed by an event that took place years before and in a hangar 6,000 miles away.

*   *   *

Passengers, mainly oilmen awaiting flights, clustered by the steamy windows of the terminal and watched the red and white airliner hurl herself down the runway from their left, trailing billowing clouds of spray in her wake. As she came closer there were puzzled murmurings from the watchers.

By now her nose should be up and the propellers dragging her into the sky. The murmurings grew louder and more alarmed.

'Kilo-Foxtrot' was level with the terminal, but her nose-wheel was still firmly on the ground!

'Oh Christ, she's not going to make it!' someone shouted.

Mesmerized by the impending tragedy, no one seemed able to look away as the aircraft hurtled towards the end of the runway. Three hundred yards from the end there was a sudden lull as the throttles were slammed shut and puffs of smoke trailed from the wheels as she braked hard.

But it was too late – five seconds and 350 yards too late. Great clods of earth flew in the air as the 748 careered over 130 yards of heath beyond the runway threshold and tore across the perimeter road that curls around the aerodrome's eastern boundary. Still travelling at 103 miles per hour, she slammed over a 15-inch drop on the seaward side of the road, hitting the ground again with such force that the undercarriage legs and propellers began to buckle and disintegrate.

One last terrible barrier lay in her path before she inevitably plunged into the heaving whitecaps of the North Sea . . . rows of 'dragon's teeth' – concrete blocks installed on the shoreline to disperse waves and prevent coastal erosion. The rest of the buckled undercarriage sheared on impact with the first row of immovable blocks. With a tearing scream she was disembowelled as, port wing low, nose down, she skidded into the sea at more than 100 miles per hour.

A mighty splash blotted her from sight as she ploughed through the water for a further 60 yards before coming to rest, beginning to sink immediately. When the blustery wind tore aside the curtains of hanging spray all that remained in view was 'Kilo-Foxtrot's' tail, marking her grave in 3 fathoms of water.

Utter, naked panic engulfed the passenger cabin as the aircraft smashed through the 'dragon's teeth' and hit the water. In an instant the port wing had gone, ripped away at its root by the impact, and her backbone broke, tearing an even wider gap in her belly through which torrents of seawater roared with brutal and terrifying force. In the darkness and confusion, 44 frightened men, cursing and lashing out wildly, fought to save themselves from the horror of drowning – kicking and elbowing, literally climbing over each other to reach the door or emergency exits. Unlike many crashes, the Dan-Air machine's plunge into the sea was survivable – indeed, everyone on board *had* survived the impact with a variety of minor injuries.

Most were certainly fit enough to join in the brawl to escape. Through the clamour came a clear treble voice, calling insistently for attention and urging calm on the cursing, heaving mass of oilmen. It was that of Liz Cowe, sternly rebuking the panic-stricken and desperately seeking to restore calm as she struggled to open the door.

When it finally swung open she remained at her post, calmly fastening others into their lifejackets and helping them towards the exits, the very substance of her safety briefing that had been received with such scant attention only minutes earlier. Fighting to bring the struggling mob to some semblance of order, she handed out lifejackets and guided men into the sea. Among them was Captain John Finney, a 38-year-old helicopter pilot.

'Without that girl I would not be alive,' he said. 'I owe her everything. All hell had broken loose and men were scrambling about trying to get out. Before I could grab a lifejacket, the people behind forced me through the emergency exit and into the water. It was very cold. I tried swimming for the shore, but wasn't making any progress. I was getting desperate and began to fear I would drown when I spotted the girl – helping support a man who was lying in the water in a lifejacket. She realized that one jacket wouldn't support three of us so she let go. The next I knew, she had somehow got hold of the only lifejacket still floating and was inflating it. Instead of keeping it herself, she made me take it.'

Captain Finney was fortunate. Others, still trapped inside, drowned as the water level rose. Among them were the two pilots. They died trying to escape through an open cockpit window. Even those who had got out were not safe. Several drowned in the heaving waves, some only yards from the shore. Two or three managed to clamber onto the rear fuselage or tailplane – only to be dashed back into the sea by breaking waves.

In the space of a few minutes 17 men perished. Thirty others – among them the gallant Liz Cowe – managed to make it to the rocky shore, slipping and stumbling through the weed-coated 'dragon's teeth', that final treacherous barrier which had ripped the guts out of 'Kilo-Foxtrot', robbing her of precious minutes of buoyancy that might have saved the rest.

*   *   *

The three men plodded down the length of Runway 09, heads bent as their eyes scanned the tyre-scarred concrete for some clue to the mystery of why a perfectly serviceable aircraft, manned by a competent crew and powered by two healthy engines should defy the laws of aerodynamics by remaining stubbornly on the ground while travelling at – and beyond – the speed when she should have taken off.

One was the Airport Commandant; the other two were William Tench, Chief Inspector of Accidents; and Colin Allen, one of his senior inspectors. It was midday on Wednesday, 1 August – 19 hours after the tragedy. If they raised their eyes, they could see the shattered fuselage of the 748, still carrying some of its cargo of dead, being hauled ashore by bulldozer.

'When we found the 748's tyre marks we were surprised,' Bill Tench recalled. 'Long after V1 – the last point at which take-off could have been safely aborted – they veered off to the left and it became clear that the nosewheel had still been in contact with the runway, way after the time it should have been in the air.

'Even beyond the runway it had been cutting a deep rut in the soft earth. I said to Colin Allen; "I hope to God he remembered to take the control lock off." But I immediately rejected the idea. Pilots just don't make that sort of mistake. It is unthinkable. So then I began to think that something must have been wrong with the elevator.'

That evening, Tench flew back to London. With him, sitting in a bucket of seawater to prevent corrosion, was 'Kilo-Foxtrot's' flight data recorder. But when it was played back it solved no mysteries. It merely showed that the aircraft had reached a maximum speed of 135 miles per hour – 21 miles per hour faster than take-off speed before crashing. It also confirmed Tench's observation that she had swerved to port as the pilot tried to steer away from the sea.

Beyond that it revealed nothing out of the ordinary. Air traffic had received no last-second message; nor was the 748 equipped with a cockpit voice recorder to enable investigators to listen to the last words of the two pilots. With his team still putting the jigsaw together in the Shetlands, Bill Tench's thoughts turned once again to the subject of locked controls.

Unlike larger aircraft, HS 748s are not fitted with hydraulic controls, being small enough to function with a system of cables and pulleys running from the cockpit to elevators, rudder and ailerons – 'stick and string' pilots call it, and it has served aircraft well since the days of the Wright Brothers.

No other arrangement gives the pilot the same 'feel' for his machine, but it has a disadvantage. If cockpit controls can move control surfaces, then control surfaces can move controls. If a stationary or slow-taxiing aircraft is hit by a gust of wind, control surfaces can flap violently, transmitting the movement along the cables and causing the rudder bar or control column to react with equal violence. More than one pilot has received a broken arm or leg from the unexpected whiplash. So 'stick and string' aircraft have gust-locks, designed to hold control surfaces rigid until the moment the pilot disengages the device just before take-off. In the pre-take-off checklist, the catechism spoken between pilot and copilot, almost the last call is: 'Gust-locks off. Check full and free movement of controls.'

Therein lay the true enigma of the Sumburgh tragedy, for Tench knew from witnesses that the pilots *had* turned their controls this way and that as a final physical check that

213

the gust-locks were disengaged. Yet at some time between them and reaching take-off speed something had caused the elevators to seize up.

Many hours were spent examining the flying controls, cables and pulleys and in combing the wreckage for some loose foreign object which might have jammed the system. There was nothing.

The tailplane and elevator hinges were searched minutely for some mark that might indicate that a stone or other object had been flung up to lodge in the gap and prevent them hingeing properly. Nothing.

Engines, internal hydraulics, fuel lines, control cables . . . all had been in perfect working order until the moment 'Kilo-Foxtrot' had charged uncontrollably off the end of Runway 09. Inexorably, the investigators were drawn back to the gust-locks.

The lever that operates them sits between the two pilots on the right of the throttle quadrant. Forward is 'off'; backwards, 'on'. To prevent accidental movement it is necessary to lift the lever with some force – as when selecting reverse gear with some cars – before it can be pushed forwards or backwards. As an additional safety device, it is impossible to open the throttle wide on more than one engine when the lock is engaged.

Sherlock Holmes's maxim was: *If you have eliminated the impossible then that which remains, however improbable, must be the answer.* Was it impossible – or merely improbable – that despite these fail-safe devices, despite the certainty that the pilots *had* proved the full and free movement of controls while lining up, that somehow the gust-lock had re-engaged between brakes off and 'VR'? With few other avenues of exploration remaining, the investigators had to upgrade the gust-lock theory from 'impossible' to 'improbable'.

The whole system was stripped down to its component parts for the engineers to go over with their magnifying glasses and micrometers. It was then, while examining a small strip of metal, that they finally unravelled the mystery, identifying the culprit as an unknown Argentinian mechanic who had done a hasty and shoddy repair job some time between 1962, when the then new 748 had been sold to Aerolineas Argentinas, and 1977 when she had come into the possession of Dan-Air from another Argentinian company, Yacimientos Petroliferos Fiscales.

The component he repaired, presumably to compensate for wear and tear, was the gate-plate. It was an integral part of the gust-lock safety mechanism, indeed the very part designed specifically to prevent the lever from being depressed at any stage of its fore-and-aft travel other than the wider 'on' or 'off' slots at either end of the gate. The job was a lash-up, using a home-made plate that did not conform to Hawker Siddeley specifications. It allowed the lever to be depressed *before* it reached the 'off' slot prior to take-off.

The result was lethal. Roy Wells, receiving the order 'Gust-locks off' would have lifted the lever out of the 'on' slot and pushed it forward, conditioned to believe that he would be able to depress it only when it reached the 'off' position. The likelihood is that he pressed down before it was level with the 'off' slot. Feeling it sink home, he would naturally assume it was in the correct position . . . an assumption reinforced when the temporary disengagement of the lock made it possible to exercise the 'full and free' movement of the control surfaces. Worst of all, depressing the lever in the wrong position overrode the safety baulk designed to prevent full power being fed to more than one engine while the gust-lock was 'on'.

With the knowledge that he had full movement of controls and power to both engines, Captain Watson let the brakes go and began to roll down Runway 09.

Then, at some moment during the next 23 seconds, came the faintest of clicks as the barely freed elevator lock slipped back into place . . .

17

Conflict on Flight BE 548

Young Trevor Burke, negotiating patches of mud as he picked his way along the footpath near the reservoir, didn't spare an upward glance as the aircraft roared overhead. Living, as he did, beneath the noisy airspace of London Heathrow, the world's busiest international airport, the endless aircraft movements were, to the 13-year-old, no more remarkable than the constant shuttle of red London buses on local roads. Not that there was anything to see anyway. It was a grey, gusty day with eight-eighths cloudbase at 1,000 feet. Four hundred feet lower, other patches of cloud sailed on the 20 miles per hour south-west wind. The time: 5.10 p.m. Date: Sunday, 18 June 1972. Location: King George V Reservoir on the south-west boundary of the airport.

As the tumult grew louder the boy cocked his head in puzzlement. There was something about the sound that seemed wrong . . . by now he should be hearing an ear-racking roar as the invisible airliner thrusted upwards for height.

Instead, the sound was coming towards him!

An indistinct shadow swam into focus in the grey underbelly of the cloudbase, dropping more clearly into sight among the drifting patches of cumulus below. Automatically, with an ease born of long experience, the teenager noted the three tail-mounted engines and identified them as those of a Trident, distinctive in the livery of British European Airways. All that was familiar enough. What was not was the attitude of the aircraft. Her long, mullet-like snout was high,

216

angled for climbing, her three engines were howling, yet the big, swept-wing aircraft was sinking fast, waffling through the air as she fell towards the grey waters of the reservoir.

The terrified boy could even see her identification letters, G-ARPI, as he stood rigid with shock, watching her drop over Staines Moor on course for the busy A30 and the streets of Staines beyond. She passed a few feet above the dual carriageway, barely clearing an overhead power line, and slammed down tail-first into a triangular-shaped recreation ground beside a factory. With a din like some monstrous thunderclap, the Trident was torn apart by the impact and the peaceful playing field vanished in a rolling avalanche of debris, flying earth and cartwheeling pieces of luggage. The roar of her disintegration seemed to last an eternity, but at last there was an awful stillness, broken only by the cries of birds fleeing in alarm, then the billowing pall of dust and smoke was wafted away by the wind, revealing a nightmare scene of carnage and destruction.

With a whimper of horror, Trevor Burke began to run as he had never run before . . .

*　　　*　　　*

Just 150 seconds before she fell into that Middlesex field, Flight BE 548 for Brussels had surged forward as the brakes were released and had accelerated westwards on Runway 28R. Forty-four seconds later, her spinning wheels parted company with the tarmac and she thrust herself upwards into the murky cloudbase. Half a minute passed, then she slanted into a 20-degree bank to port – the start of a climbing turn to the south that would ultimately take her on to an easterly heading towards the English Channel and the Belgian coast.

At her controls was Captain Stanley Key who, at 51, was one of BEA's most senior and experienced pilots. On the flight deck with him were no fewer than three other company pilots . . . yet, despite all this expertise, within 1½ minutes of the start of the take-off run 'Papa-India' was allowed to fall out of the sky.

All four pilots died instantly as she flew into the ground at 155 miles per hour. Two stewards, a stewardess and 111 passengers were killed in the same instant. One hundred and eighteen dead . . . it was a tragedy of huge proportions – until that time Britain's worst-ever airline disaster.

. A full-scale public enquiry was ordered by the Heath Government. Under the chairmanship of Mr Justice Geoffrey Lane, a High Court judge and wartime bomber pilot, it began on 20 November at London's Piccadilly Hotel, ending on 25 January the following year. During that time 13 lawyers and 67 witnesses appeared. More than two million words of evidence were recorded in the 83-page report that emerged for the then Trade and Industry Secretary, the Right Honourable Peter Walker. The story it told was a disquieting catalogue of bungling, vendetta, misjudgment and fatal chance.

*　　*　　*

That evening, as fleets of ambulances recovered the bodies to ferry them to a makeshift mortuary, a team of AIB experts began picking their way grimly through the torn pieces of wreckage. They quickly found the two flight data recorders upon whose wire spools were etched every detail of the Trident's final 150-second flight. With them they also unearthed the quick-access cassette recorder, BEA's own device designed to give a basic read-out while the more complex 'black box' recordings were being analysed.

Within hours of the crash, using BEA's flight recorder unit at Heathrow, the first disturbing facts were beginning to emerge, a series of errors upon errors that had the experts shaking their heads in disbelief. Very soon they had the answer to the question 'What?' The question 'Why?' took much, much longer and will never be answered in full.

The pattern of any take-off is determined by a complex mathematical formula revolving around weight, speed, barometric pressure and weather conditions. There was considerable turbulence around Heathrow on the afternoon of 18

June, 'Papa-India' was carrying almost a full complement of passengers and was loaded, in addition, with almost 8½ tons of fuel. For her, the formula dictated an initial climbing speed of 203 miles per hour. Yet the 'black box' showed that she was moving at only 195 miles per hour when the automatic pilot was engaged at the unusually low altitude of 355 feet.

Aircraft are at their most vulnerable at low speed and so, as a safety device, Tridents are fitted with 'droops', retractable slats along the leading edges of the wing which, when extended for take-off, make the wing bigger, so giving more lift in the crucial moments of climb. Their use improves the stalling speed by as much as 35 miles per hour. 'Papa-India's' droops should have remained extended until she had passed 3,000 feet and had accelerated to 260 miles per hour. Then, and only then, should they have been retracted to make the wing 'clean' for cruising flight. One hundred and fourteen seconds after she began to roll, the Trident was at a mere 1,772 feet, flying at only 186 miles per hour – 74 miles an hour less than the safe retraction speed.

Yet in that instant, inexplicably, someone on the flight deck moved the lever that retracted the droops.

The effect was to kick 'Papa-India's' legs from under her. As the droops slid back into their housings, thus diminishing the wing area, the aircraft was left with insufficient lift to keep her aloft. She began to wallow into a stall. Even after this appalling misjudgment she might still have been saved – by a built-in safety device called a 'stick-pusher'. Standard on all Tridents, this operates automatically when the speed is dangerously low, literally nudging the control column forward and instantly disengaging the automatic pilot. The effect is twofold – first, it puts the aircraft's nose down, allowing her to build up a few precious knots of airspeed; second, it is an unmistakable warning to the pilot that his speed has fallen off to a perilous rate. The recording showed that 'Papa-India's' stick-pusher shoved the nose down just two seconds after the droops were retracted. Incredibly, this vital warning was ignored.

What *should* have followed was that the aircraft should have been held straight and level, the throttles opened and the droops re-engaged to prevent a stall. What actually happened was that the nose was allowed to rise again and no move was made either to open the throttles or to re-engage the droops. Inevitably, 'Papa-India' mushed back towards the stall. Again the stick-pusher gave clear warning eight seconds later, ramming the pilots' control columns forward. Again, there was no reaction on the flight deck. Three seconds later came another firm push. That, too, produced no response. That three such clear warnings of impending doom could be ignored was astonishing enough, but the folly of what happened next was almost beyond belief.

One second after the third stick-push, someone on the flight deck simply switched off the mechanism.

'Papa-India' reared her nose up into a full-scale aerodynamic stall from which, at that height, there could be no possible recovery.

Less than half a minute later she hit the ground.

*   *   *

As the analysts checked and re-checked the recordings of that extraordinary sequence of events, other AIB men continued to pick their way through the debris in the hunt for clues. Still others were interviewing BEA aircrew who had been in the crewroom with Captain Key and his colleagues minutes before take-off.

At the same time, RAF aviation pathologists were conducting autopsies on the four men who had been on 'Papa-India's' flight deck: Captain Key; his copilot, Jeremy Keighley (22); Second Officer Simon Ticehurst (24); and Captain John Collins, a BEA pilot who had elected to sit 'up front' while travelling as a passenger.

Already the analysts had *their* startling data to process on their computers. Now it was the turn of the other investigators – and very quickly each group came up with information that ranged from the disturbing to the downright sinister. In the cockpit they found Second Officer Ticehurst's table, a small folding flap on which to rest his log and other documents while working in the air. Much of its surface was covered with offensive scribbles and graffiti.

In large capitals, one read: 'KEY MUST GO.'

Beneath, probably in a different hand, was written: 'Yes, but where?' to which someone had added: 'Down the drain to BOAC. Anywhere will do!'

Another scribble read: 'Bloody stirrer!'

However, it was the last scrawl that came as a bombshell: *When Stanley Key dies who will be God's next representative to BEA?*

Stanley Key *had* died, and with him 117 other men, women and children. The graffiti added an entirely new dimension to the mystery, especially when many other abusive anti-Key scrawls were discovered on the flight decks of other Tridents in BEA's fleet.

A handwriting expert was hastily called in. The AIB men redoubled their interviews with other pilots and aircrew – and soon found themselves embroiled in the politics of a long-standing dispute between BEA management and pilots. The row was over pay and conditions, and some members of the British Airline Pilots' Association (BALPA) were operating a limited work-to-rule. Captain Key, however, had been firmly opposed to any industrial action. He had not been afraid to say so and had, in fact, busied himself lobbying support from others against his more militant colleagues. His action had earned him enemies. How many can be judged by the fact that the handwriting expert eventually analysed *nine* different hands in the graffiti throughout the Trident fleet.

The culprits, to this day, have not been identified. Close on the heels of the graffiti revelations came a new drama – reports by aircrew that Stanley Key had been involved in a bitter, blazing quarrel with a first officer from another crew in the BEA crewroom shortly before the departure of 'Papa-India'. The subject had been the BALPA dispute. The other man had asked, sarcastically, how Key's efforts to drum up opposition to it were progressing.

Roaring with rage, the senior pilot exploded. At least one witness described it as the most violent quarrel he had ever heard, though Key had calmed down soon afterwards and apologized for his outburst.

Jeremy Keighley, the quiet and diffident copilot – about to make his first flight with the irascible Key – was a witness to that row and was shaken by the sheer force of his Captain's anger. Suspecting a weak link, the AIB men delved into the 22-year-old's records. His reports from flying school and BEA training school showed he was a slow learner and under-confident. 'He will need careful watching,' said one. Another read: '. . . he was slow to react to an emergency. He lacked initiative.' It was also revealed that Keighley had received no in-flight stall recovery training. His only experience of flying a Trident out of a stall had been at the controls of a ground simulator.

The last piece of the jigsaw slotted into place when the pathologist completed his post-mortem of Captain Key. The bluff and seemingly hearty pilot had in fact been a very sick man, prey to a condition which, unknown to him and his doctors, had been slowly developing for more than 30 years. It was a severe heart condition called arteriosclerosis – fatty hardening of the arteries. So bad it that in places the arteries' bore had been reduced by 70 per cent, seriously restricting the flow of blood.

Stanley Key, the doctors concluded, had probably been doomed anyway. For in the left coronary artery they found a tear in the arterial wall, causing a haemorrhage which had occurred sometime between two hours and one minute before 'Papa-India' plunged into the playing field. The cause was stress, and Key had been subjected to more than his fair share of stress that day during the brief but incandescent row in the crewroom and perhaps by a glimpse of the offensive scrawls in the cockpit.

No one can ever be certain what happened during those fateful 150 seconds, for 'Papa-India' was not equipped with a cockpit voice recorder to log the final words of her crew. But the detailed and painstaking work of the accident investigators and other experts paints for us the probable scenario . . .

Captain Key, his dangerous heart condition inflamed by the row and the sight of the cruel scrawls, began suffering chest pains during the critical moments of take-off, pains so severe that his normally first-class judgement was badly affected.

Why else should such a competent pilot retract (or order Keighley to retract) the droops at a speed guaranteed to put the aircraft into a stall? Why else was the flight pattern flown at consistently and perilously low speeds? Why else was the stick-pusher warning thrice ignored? Why else was that same safety device – the last hope of salvation – dumped at such a critical time?

And while all this was happening, the only man with access to the dual controls was the shy, under-confident, inexperienced Jeremy Keighley. Of him the official report said:

It was the worst of bad luck that he should have been in the second seat. His witnessing of the crewroom incident . . . can have done nothing but harm to his self-confidence. His natural tendency towards self-effacement would not have encouraged him to question the actions of his captain . . . particularly a captain with whom he had never flown before and his slower than average reactions would probably not have been a match for the sudden and alarming events on the flight deck.

Bad temper, bad health and bad judgment – all these factors came together with fatal consequences a third of a mile above Staines Reservoir on that Sunday evening in 1972.

The last and most deadly factor was the bad luck of Stanley Key's heart attack. For from that moment on, time had run out for the 118 souls aboard Flight BE 548.